P9-DGO-045

DO
COOL
SH*T

DO COOL SH✲T

(QUIT YOUR DAY JOB,
START YOUR OWN BUSINESS, AND
LIVE HAPPILY EVER AFTER)

MIKI AGRAWAL

DISCARDED

SCHENECTADY CO PUBLIC LIBRARY

HARPER
BUSINESS

An Imprint of HarperCollins*Publishers*
www.harpercollins.com

DO COOL SH*T. Copyright © 2013 by Miki Agrawal. All rights reserved. Printed in the United States of America. No part of this book may be used or reproduced in any manner whatsoever without written permission except in the case of brief quotations embodied in critical articles and reviews. For information, address HarperCollins Publishers, 10 East 53rd Street, New York, NY 10022.

HarperCollins books may be purchased for educational, business, or sales promotional use. For information, please e-mail the Special Markets Department at SPsales@harpercollins.com.

FIRST EDITION

Designed by Renato Stanisic

Creative direction for illustrations by Radha Agrawal. Illustrations courtesy of Guillaume Bracquemond.

Library of Congress Cataloging-in-Publication Data

Agrawal, Miki.
Do cool sh*t : quit your day job, start your own business, and live happily ever after / Miki Agrawal.—First edition.
pages cm
ISBN 978-0-06-226153-3
1. Career development. 2. Young adults. 3. Job satisfaction. 4. Entrepreneurship.
5. New business enterprises. 6. Success in business. 7. Agrawal, Miki. I. Title.
HF5381.A535 2013
658.1'1—dc23
2013010176

13 14 15 16 17   OV/RRD   10 9 8 7 6 5 4 3 2 1

FIRST, THIS BOOK IS DEDICATED TO YOU.

Thank you for wanting to do cool shit in this lifetime.
It's a short one, so we need to make it count!

Second, this book is dedicated to baby Emi, my first niece and the very
first baby to be born in the next generation of my family.

Emi, may your journey be thoughtful, courageous, and without hesitation.
I am so looking forward to watching you choose your own adventure.
I will be right next to you, cheering you on!

(ACKNOWLEDGMENTS)

I would love to give my deepest gratitude to the following people:

Mama and Daddy—for marching to your own drums and bravely coming to this country on your own and making the American dream come true. Thank you for thinking about us before thinking about yourselves. Also for creating Agra-Palooza; we're cool because of you.

Yuri (a.k.a. Dr. Agrawal)—for being the most admired big sister and setting the bar at an unreachable level and for becoming a surgeon and allowing our Asian parents to be satisfied with one doctor in the house, thus allowing Rads and I to pursue our dreams. This journey was made possible because of you! ☺

Benny Z—for getting my big sis pregnant. And for helping save our planet from extinction.

Radha (a.k.a. Rads)—for our egg splitting and for giving me someone fun to play with for a few months while I was chilling in the womb. Oh, and also for being a constant source of competitive inspiration (and being my best friend). I also happen to think that the Super Sprowtz are the raddest bunch ever.

Andrew Horn—for being my rock and my light, and for teaching me the important lessons of slowing down and appreciation.

Colleen Lawrie—for editing this crazy book and for being *super* patient with me. You're a saint!

Michele Rubin—for kicking ass and helping me get a book deal in two weeks flat.

Antonia Dunbar—for going through each chapter with me and editing this book as I wrote it. You've been an incredible friend and business partner; the future is bright for us!

Sam Horn—for supporting this book and for helping me get the book proposal to a place where I could sell it! And for producing a magical son.

Zach Iscol and the Iscol family—for your endless support; for putting up with your little hellions for a very, very long time; and for being catalysts to some of our "life breaks."

Zach Lynd—for being a first-class confidant and for designing a restaurant brand that I am truly proud of.

John Arena—for being my sensei and perspective-check in all my crisis moments.

To the *WILD* team—you guys are so good-looking and make me so happy going to the best restaurant in New York (and Vegas!).

To all of my incredible friends—"I am who I am because of who we all are" (Ubuntu).

Thank you all from the bottom of my heart.

(CONTENTS)

(FOREWORD)

I've never met anyone quite like Miki.

Actually, that's not true.

I also know her identical twin sister, Radha, who looks a lot like Miki, but that's beside the point.

When Miki first asked me to write the foreword for her book, I was a little reluctant. I told her I wanted to wait and read a draft of the entire book first before committing to write anything.

So after a few weeks, she sent me the rest of her book. And I procrastinated and didn't read it for a few more weeks, until one day when I was getting on a long flight from Los Angeles to Munich I decided to finally start reading the book.

To my surprise, on that flight, I ended up finishing the entire book.

Even though I've hung out with Miki many times as friends, and we are about to partner together professionally as she opens up her pizza place in downtown Vegas (it's an important part of our Downtown Project revitalization efforts), I never knew her full story before, or really understood what drove her. I guess I just assumed she was born that way.

As I read through Miki's journey, I found myself nodding and agreeing with a lot of the lessons learned and the advice and tips she gives.

Her stories are great stories, not just for entrepreneurs, but really for anyone who wants to lead a more fulfilling life.

In a lot of ways, Miki is like a little sister to me. So I guess this is my roundabout way of saying that although I was at first a little reluctant to write the foreword (as any big brother that likes to tease his little sister would be), I was pleasantly surprised and am really proud of her for writing this book. It's actually a really good book.

Don't let the fact that it's an easy read fool you. It's full of great insights that could have a transformative effect on your own life.

And, Miki—no, this does not mean I will stop teasing you.

Tony Hsieh
Zappos.com CEO
Author of the number one *New York Times*
bestseller *Delivering Happiness*
DowntownProject.com

(PREFACE)

To ensure that this book has found its way into your hands for the *right* reasons, please ask yourself, "Do I fall into one or more of these following categories?"

- I don't want to work a day job in a "respectable industry" just to make a buck.
- I want to have the social life I always dreamed about.
- I want to get the blessing of my parents/significant others to chase my *real* passion.
- I actually don't know what my *real* passion is yet, and I really want to figure it out.
- I have a really great idea and want to start a business but I have no clue where to begin.
- The books that *do* teach me how to start a business put me to sleep after page three.
- I want to raise money for my business, but I have never raised money before.
- I'm sick of feeling self-conscious when I walk into a room full of strangers, and I want to know how to break into a new circle with sparkle and confidence.

- I'm done going to bars and watching football for ten hours on weekends with my college friends who drink their faces off, and I want more.
- I want to build a new community of friends who challenge, support, and inspire me.
- I realize that there are people in my life who aren't helping me be my best; they may even be holding me back. I want to surround myself with the right people.

If you nodded your head to any one of those statements, buckle up and get ready to do the coolest shit you've ever done.

From now on, you will no longer feel envious of others who "have the perfect life" or intimidated by anyone trying to keep you from your perfect life. You will have the courage, clarity, and confidence to become authentic, empowered, and actualized—the best version of yourself you could ever imagine.

DO
COOL
SH*T

IS "SUCCESS" *REALLY* WHAT YOU THINK IT IS?

Why Do You Want to Be Successful?

Success is not final, failure is not fatal; it is the courage to continue that counts.
—Winston Churchill

Miami, Florida—April 8, 2011, 11:55 a.m.

The instructions were very clear on the invitation: the cruise ship would set sail at noon on Friday. If I missed it . . . well, I would miss the whole trip.

I was determined to beat my internal time clock. I'm half Indian (from India), and for those who don't know, following "Indian standard time" means showing up a minimum of an hour late, sometimes two. Thankfully my other half is Japanese, and "Japanese standard time" means you show up ten minutes early, following the old Marine Corps adage that if you're not ten minutes early, you're ten minutes late.

As I sprinted through the streets of downtown Miami toward the docks, smoke could have been coming off the wheels of my luggage. I needed to make this ship. If I had to, I would take a running start, *Mission: Impossible* style, and plummet headfirst into the freezing water to catch that vessel. No stuntman; just me. In a sundress.

I had traveled all around the world. My passport held stamps from India, Japan, Africa, Australia, all over South America and Europe. But up to this point, I had never been on a cruise, and I had certainly never been on any trip that put me in the same place as one thousand of the top entrepreneurs in the world.

In other words, this was a trip of a lifetime and there was no f-ing way I was going to miss it.

Off in the distance, I could see the faint outline of this *massive* ship that looked about to set sail. A horn blared. I had already been sprinting for fifteen minutes, with my bags scratching my legs and the straps cutting through the skin on my shoulders.

I got closer . . . I was so out of breath . . . closer . . . there's the ramp! Get on the ramp! Another horn. They're *leaving*? Wait!

I made it with just enough time for me to hurdle the rope and land on the boat safely before the walkway was removed.

Why did I have to make this so hard for myself? Every time I go anywhere, my life turns into an action movie where I'm sprinting around, when it could very easily be a nice, slow-paced romantic French film. If only I'd leave one hour earlier.

I wiped the sweat off my brow, readjusted my bags, and casually strolled onto the deck.

As I stepped onto the first level of the ship after checking in, I couldn't believe who I saw.

It was Richard Branson, my entrepreneurial hero. He was sitting at the bar, sipping a drink and regaling eager young entrepreneurs with a story. His white-blond hair blew gently in the wind. This scene was the perfect first mental snapshot—one that I'd remember for years to come. I was so excited to see him; I tripped over my heel, caught myself just in time, and kept walking. I decided I was too flustered by my harried arrival to meet him yet (and I was still sweating my ass off from running).

The boat was magnificent. There were five floors and two gorgeous outdoor levels where everyone could enjoy the waves and the sun during the day and the stars at night. There was a big DJ station and dance floor on the second level, and I knew immediately that's where I would end up every night. People were milling about with their luggage, finding their cabins and exploring just like I was.

I spotted Tony Hsieh (CEO of Zappos.com), Blake Mycoskie (founder of TOMS), Gary Vaynerchuk (founder of Wine Library), and a slew of other founders of leading nonprofits like Charity: Water, Pencils of Promise, and Invisible Children. It was incredible!

I grabbed my cell phone out of my pocket to call Radha (my twin sister) to give her the play-by-play, but as I tried to dial, I realized my phone didn't work. One of the ship workers saw me fussing with my phone, so he approached me and told me that cell phones didn't work on the boat.

Really? So nobody would be able to make any calls? That meant that we would actually have one less distraction while we were communicating (and hopefully collaborating) with one another for four straight days. I loved that idea! What better way for fresh entrepreneurial ideas to be shared than without any technological aid, just through words, eye contact, and smiles?

I pulled out my four-day itinerary and saw that I had to be in the auditorium for the opening session at 4:00 p.m., during which Richard Branson would be speaking. Wow, Summit Series, who put together this cruise, didn't waste any time bringing out their superstars!

I was also pumped to read that the Roots were the cruise's house band and would be playing every single night along with big-name DJs like Pretty Lights and Axwell from Swedish House Mafia! Unreal.

I could attend morning yoga sessions, as well as large and small talks on everything from environmental and social innovation to personal empowerment—there was just so much to do! I was so impressed with the execution of this event.

Summit at Sea was an invite-only event, so I felt grateful to be invited. I had started a successful small business at age twenty-six, and the point of the summit was to bring together up-and-coming entrepreneurs and young talent with established industry leaders.

I played back in my mind the events that led me to be on this boat. My entrepreneurial adventure began with a frustrating recurring stomachache that sparked the idea to open the first lactose-intolerant-friendly farm-to-table pizza and local craft beer restaurant in New York City. We called it *SLICE* (now called *WILD)* and it serves farm-fresh pizzas with no hormones, additives, or other crap in it, and supports local farms and businesses.

I had opened my first restaurant on the Upper East Side of Manhattan at the end of 2005 on a shoestring budget, and I called on every favor I could to make it happen. I was twenty-six years old and had never worked in the restaurant business, but I was convinced that a farm-fresh healthy pizza concept was going to change the way people thought about their favorite guilty pleasure. At the time, it was still early in the game for *local* and *organic* to be mainstream terms, and it was a struggle at first to convince people that healthy pizza actually didn't taste like cardboard. We were one of the first alternative pizzerias in New York to offer gluten-free and vegan options, and being a pioneer in this industry certainly didn't make the journey an easy one.

During the cruise, I was excited to learn as much as I could and meet as many people as I could, especially the great leaders who I had admired from afar for so long!

One of the greats on the cruise was Tony Hsieh, the CEO of Zappos .com. I figured since he was a guy who started two successful businesses and sold them by the time he was thirty-six for a collective $1.4 billion, he probably had some *good* stories to tell and some even better advice for a young entrepreneur like me.

Around sundown, I saw that he was sitting at the bar on the second floor of the boat and quite a few people were milling around him, trying to speak with him. I'm not usually the shyest person in a room, but it took me a few circles around the bar to muster up the courage to walk over to him.

Why was I so nervous? Why couldn't I just go up to him and say something? He was a human being just like me. But the fact that he had achieved so much at such a young age was incredibly intimidating to me.

As I passed by him on my laps and watched him make small talk with a bunch of people, I made a call: I decided not to say anything to him at all. I could tell from his interactions with other people that *he* was shy. He liked to talk to people for sure, but he had a lovable awkwardness about him and you could tell that he preferred to listen more than talk. He seemed like the kind of guy who would be more open in a one-on-one setting, so instead of adding my small talk to the rest he would endure that night, I decided to stand across the bar from him, stare at him until he made eye contact with me (who cares if I looked like a complete stalker?), smile, and wave. He smiled back.

And that was it. It didn't matter that he didn't remember me at all—I had the smile, which meant I had the in! I knew that I would get in touch with him when I was back in New York. (He had put his e-mail address down at the end of one of his presentations on the boat, and I had it securely in my notebook.) Mission accomplished.

The rest of the trip was a dream. It was one of the first times I had met so many like-minded people, all wanting the same thing: to create new businesses that had cultural and social relevance, and with real societal impact.

I tagged sharks for science; had in-depth conversations with artists, poets, top entrepreneurs, and change makers; and I danced every night with my new friends on the boat's main deck, with the Roots jamming away.

. . . .

The day after I got back from the cruise, I sent Tony an e-mail with the subject heading: "Great meeting you on the boat at Summit!" (though we technically hadn't met and he probably had zero recollection of who I was).

In the body of the e-mail, I wrote a few sentences about me and briefly described my farm-to-table pizza concept, and then I mentioned my new social enterprise called THINX, a technologically advanced pair of beautiful, leak- and stain-resistant underwear for girls to wear during their periods. THINX also solves a global menstruation management problem for girls in the developing world (clearly unrelated to pizza). I told him that I would love to speak with him about the new idea and see if a partnership with Zappos.com could be formed.

He responded within minutes. (He's good like that, even though he sometimes receives more than two thousand e-mails every day, as I later found out. That's what happens when you generously put your e-mail address at the end of every presentation.) He said that he would be in New York in mid-May and that he'd like to come to my restaurant.

Wait. Really?! I had to read his e-mail twice to be sure I wasn't dreaming it. I wrote him back and set up our meeting.

It had taken me a couple of years of messing up and figuring stuff out before I was able to make enough money to open up my second location in the West Village. I had always dreamed of opening a place in this beautiful part of the city, and I am incredibly proud of it, so it was quite special to arrange for Tony to meet me there.

I remember reading Tony's book, *Delivering Happiness*, in which he mentions that pizza was one of his favorite businesses as it brought back great memories from his Harvard days. It was something we had in common, and it would be a great icebreaker to begin our conversation.

The day Tony was planning to come by, I brought my partners in the THINX venture: Radha (my twin sister) and Antonia (our other partner). Just like when he was on the boat, Tony started off by observing in the corner of my restaurant, quietly listening to the three of us excitedly talk about our new business. I was so glad I brought Rads and Antonia because their presence immediately made me more comfortable and confident.

What happened at this meeting was quite special. Antonia, Rads, and I always get really excited when we talk about pretty much everything, so in this instance, the excitement caught on. We told Tony our idea for THINX; we talked about our other concept Super Sprowtz, and we talked about the restaurant, and then we talked about the Downtown Project, which was the big project that Tony was working on. By the end of our conversation, Tony had come out of his quiet shell and we were having one of those really great conversations—you know, the ones where you end up interrupting each other and going off on tangents as you get more excited. I couldn't believe how energetic Tony was—it was a much different side of him than I'd witnessed on the boat, and it was wonderful to watch.

Tony said that he was interested in supporting our new project, THINX, and connected us to his merchandising and sales team.

Hooray!

But, to my amazement, that wasn't even what he had come in to talk about.

Rather, he wanted to partner with me to open my pizza concept in Las Vegas!

His latest endeavor, the Downtown Project, is to revitalize downtown Las Vegas, and he knew that the downtown area was in desperate need of tasty, healthy eateries.

He wanted my restaurant to be an integral part of the new development. (It just goes to show you that you never know what wonderful, unexpected surprises can come from being brave and introducing yourself to new people.)

Wow. I had to take a breath. I had spent six years building my business, mostly on my own, from scratch, and I was finally getting my first big break! And it was with Tony Hsieh?! I couldn't believe it! I really do think that one of the big things that sealed the deal for him was our excitement and passion for our ideas. Genuine excitement builds believers. It just does.

Downtown Las Vegas—Six months later, 3:00 a.m.

was up late, chatting with Tony, who by now had become a good friend and business partner, and he told me that he always loves asking people this question: "Why do you want to be successful?"

Many people would answer: "Because I want to make a lot of money."

Then he would ask, "Why?"

They would respond, "Because I want to pay off my loans or I want to buy a really great car or house."

Not satisfied yet, he would ask again, prompting them to really think about it. Eventually, he would get down to the real reason: "Because I want to be happy."

When you ask someone "Why?" enough times, the answer most often ends up with "Because I want to be happy." Try it. It works!

And my own definition of success has certainly changed over the years. When I finished college, it was financial freedom. I had student loans to pay off and not much in the way of savings, so I became an investment banker in an effort to make all the money I could and ended up wanting to gouge my eyes out instead. After that tough experience, I learned the hard way that you *can* find ways to enjoy what you do, work with people who you like, *and* make money rather than working simply to be financially free.

Later, after I started my business, my definition of success changed again and became "freedom of time." I was bound with both hands to my business and I never saw my friends and family and could never take any time off. Being able to bring someone on who could operate my restaurant was the best thing I had ever done. Now that I am no longer the only one keeping my business afloat, I can think about forming strategic partnerships to grow it and think about the bigger picture.

Now my definition of success is living to my full potential. I want it all. I know now from experience that it's possible to have a growing, successful business and a passionate relationship, to be in the best shape of your life, to give back to your community, and to push your boundaries when it comes to new adventures. It took years of searching, but I think I might have figured it out. I know how to be happy.

In this book, I will show you how I did it, step by step, for my business and for my personal life.

I challenge you to ask yourself these two questions before you begin reading this book. It may seem easy at first, but when you really dig deep, the "why" is always tough.

- What is your definition of success?
- Why do *you* want to be successful?

SO . . . ARE YOU READY TO "DO COOL SHIT"?

This book is meant for those of you who want to have the greatest stories to tell. Your story will start from this very moment and when you look back at every year as it unfolds, you will say to yourself, "Wow, a lot of cool shit happened to me this year." You will smile, be excited, feel grateful . . . and then carry on doing cool shit.

I wrote this book because I wish someone had told me earlier that this kind of life was possible, and perhaps in reading this, you can find the answers I had been seeking for so long. I, for one, had been frustrated with the reading material out there. I didn't want to sit through another boring how-to business book, either from someone thirty years older than I am, to whom I couldn't relate at all, or a book that solely tackles the nuts and bolts of starting and running a business.

I wanted to have answers for people like me—the new generation of people who didn't want to follow the traditional paths of investment banking, management consulting, medicine, or law. Had I known that there was another way to approach entrepreneurship coming out of college, I would have jumped straight into it. Practical classes on starting a business were simply not taught in college, and being an entrepreneur was not even on my radar as a career option. This book is the road map that I wish I had been given when I graduated from college.

And where was the book that would show me where to find the coolest friends who were also doing the coolest shit? Or how to make room for true love in my life? These days, so many of us have thousands of online friends, but how many of them are real friends? Everyone wants to have love and feel loved. This book will show you how to get there.

I love stories. I love stories from firsthand experience and stories that have a purpose. I love stories that break things down for me in ways that I can digest and apply to my life. This is one of those books. You will walk away from each chapter with tangible takeaways and systems that you can apply in your life.

And last, this book will remind you that you have a backbone and that you are inherently strong. It will remind you that it's cool to care and be excited about ideas, it's cool to be proactive, it's cool to mess up, it's cool to work your ass off on something that is meaningful to you, and it's cool to keep trying when the odds are stacked against you.

OK, go forth! And may you bask in the journey of doing cool shit.

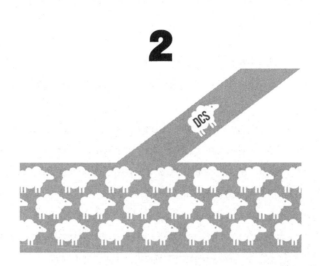

2

STRAY FROM THE GROUP

How to Make Friends in New Places and Talk to Anyone, Anywhere

Why fit in when you're born to stand out?
—Dr. Seuss

My heart was racing as I sat in the waiting room outside the director's office. What if he sent me home? I'd be the first person in the history of the Boston University London Internship Program to be sent home. But I simply couldn't stay where I was, at that office. It was worse than a horror film, and it had given me nightmares for weeks. The women I was working for were total and utter bitches, I wasn't learning anything, and of course, I wasn't getting paid. Ideally, an internship should always be akin to an apprenticeship. Yes, you bring coffee and make copies, but you're also supposed to be learning about the business, sitting in on low-level meetings, and networking. No, I decided. I would stand my ground and brace myself for the worst. I felt confident that if I was sent home, I would still have done the right thing, and I'd be able to spend my time more productively.

I think everyone should study or live abroad at some point in their lives. I was given that opportunity during my second semester of junior year of college.

I played Division I soccer for Cornell University, and at that point, soccer defined me. This sport had taught me most of my biggest life lessons—the ones all sports teach a youngster: commitment, stamina, confidence, and teamwork. But also the less obvious ones—like resilience and the value of being scrappy.

My second semester of junior year was the only time I wasn't playing soccer, so I jumped at the opportunity to try something different—to get some distance from this sport and my intense commitment to it. I was ready to fulfill the other college dream of mine: to experience, exist, and thrive in another part of the world.

I really could have picked anywhere to go study abroad. My twin sis, Rads, picked Paris. I had friends who did the Semester at Sea program. My friend Jen went to Spain. I wasn't feeling a strong draw to France or Spain (or the sea sickness of Semester at Sea), so I ended up picking a city that also happened to be strongly defined by soccer, or should I say "football": London, England. So much for taking a break from soccer!

I had always wanted to live in London. At the time, I had the biggest crush on Hugh Grant and dreamed that perhaps, while studying abroad, I would run into him in the streets by Big Ben or something and he'd ask to get a spot of tea with me. Hey, it could happen.

Another great draw was that the Boston University Internship Program's credits were accepted by Cornell and it would be a unique opportunity to study abroad and intern at a real British business. It sounded perfect for me.

I had to then convince my parents to let go of their death grip on my academic path to success, and that this was the best idea for me *and* my education. My parents came from abroad originally, so it wasn't too hard to convince them. My father came to America from India with five dollars in his pocket. My mother came from Japan and her lineage traced directly to some important Japanese samurais. (I'm part samurai! Don't mess with me.) They both bravely ventured away from their respective home countries to study abroad in America. Their one year abroad turned into a lifetime once they met and fell in love.

Regardless of my parents' wanderlust, academics have always been incredibly important to them and played a major role in our household. So I knew I had to work really hard to make them understand why I wanted to go abroad and not stay at Cornell, which would have been much more rigorous academically.

I put together a pitch presentation for my parents and worked to sell them on the idea using the following factors:

- I get to learn about a different country's culture and traditions.
- I will gain real experience in business.
- I will be forced outside my comfort zone.
- This experience would save them money.

It *is* often cheaper to study abroad for a semester than to study at a private school in the United States for that term. And wouldn't you know, the last bit was what put them over the edge. My adventure abroad was about to begin!

Do Cool Shit Takeaway
Create Your Personalized Pitch Presentation

If you *really* want to do something cool and need the support of your parents, teachers, or bosses, treat it like it's a new business idea and put together a creative and professional personalized pitch presentation around what you want to do.

> **Create a simple PowerPoint deck (ten slides or so) that covers the following:**
>
> - **What you want to do**
> - **Three to five reasons why you want to do it**
> - **Three to five ways it benefits you and them academically/ professionally/personally**
>
> **It helps to connect your dream with a dream held by the person you are pitching. It will help them to empathize with your situation and might just push them over the edge into agreeing to help.**
>   **Include lots of photos. A picture is worth a thousand words! Check out a sample pitch deck at docoolshit.org.**

With my parents' blessing, I packed my bags. I made a promise that in order to truly integrate myself, once I arrived, I wouldn't comingle with any other American students. I would entirely immerse myself in the British culture (and possibly come back to America with a hint of a British accent. I mean, Madonna managed to acquire one after only a couple of weeks there. If she could do it, so could I.).

Once I arrived at my two-bedroom flat in the posh neighborhood of South Kensington, I unpacked and made the easy walk over to the campus for orientation. I passed massive taxis driving on the "wrong" side of the street and was charmed by the quaint English cobblestoned streets. I couldn't wait to experience everything I could in this enchanting city.

As part of our orientation, we had to take a "Culture Shock" class, which was supposed to teach us what we should and shouldn't do during our semester in London. It was stuff like, "Don't go up to random British people and talk to them." They told us that British people aren't as open as Americans. "Don't talk on the tube," as the British are pin-drop quiet on the subway. Hmm—I wasn't digging the fact that the teacher was telling us what we shouldn't do. It has never been my strong suit to take orders and, anyway, shouldn't it be up to us to discover these things on our own?

I received my internship package and found out that I was going to be working with a prestigious PR firm in London. I was excited to start learning some hard business skills and gain an understanding of what public relations really was as an industry.

I was equally excited to go on the bike tour our program had organized for that afternoon, do some sightseeing of the British monuments, and spend some time in the town with a tour guide who I was sure would be equipped with a great story or seven.

Later, a group of about forty of us gathered by the bike rental place. The guide gave us one rule that we had to follow: "Don't stray from the group." No matter what, we had to stick with the group so that nobody got lost. It seemed like a reasonable request.

As we passed by Big Ben, the Tower Bridge, and the Tower of London, I pictured every romantic comedy that featured these icons and smiled. Obviously, I kept my eye out for the Notting Hill neighborhood as we rode through the city.

It was at this point that we passed by the place that would end up kick-starting my entire experience in England: Hyde Park.

It was a Sunday, and on Sundays at Hyde Park, there were about a dozen soccer games going on at any given time. Yes! Soccer! I knew where I was going to be spending my Sundays for the rest of the semester. I scanned the games and realized that there was not *one single girl* in any of the games. Did no girls play soccer in London? I decided this was a good thing. I would definitely stand out in this crowd.

I studied the groups playing on that majestic lawn and noticed that there was one group of young gentlemen that seemed particularly cool

(OK, fine, I admit it, they were hot). But they were also just playing a great technical game. They probably had dreamy accents too. As I was taking it all in, I hadn't noticed that our bike tour was quickly moving past Hyde Park. Shit! What do I do? I didn't want to lose the opportunity to potentially play soccer with a group of hot Brits!

In that instant, I had to make a game-time decision (pun intended). Do I lose the boring biker gang and meet some locals? After all, I had made a pact with myself to hang out with only Brits. A word came immediately to mind and I knew it couldn't be ignored: *regret*. I simply couldn't regret missing this incredible opportunity to meet the *very* people I came to London to meet.

I had my answer. I took a deep breath, smiled, and proceeded to ride my bike smack-dab in the middle of their game. (Who the F *does* that?)

I yelled (OK, it came out more like a shrill squeak than anything): "Excuse me! Hi! Can I talk with you guys real quick? My bike tour is leaving and I need to talk to you right away!"

These guys stopped playing, quizzically looked at one another, and finally tentatively approached me. One tall, ginger-haired guy named Ben, who I would learn was affectionately known by his friends as "Irish," was first to talk.

"You all right?" he asked.

I replied, "I just landed from New York yesterday and I play soccer in college. I want to train while I'm here, so I was wondering if I can get your numbers so can we play sometime?"

These guys were so confused. After a long and awkward pause, Irish begrudgingly gave me his number. I grabbed it out of his hand and rode off to catch up to the bike tour.

That night I called the number and Irish picked up after the third ring.

"You all right?" he asked again.

I told him I was going to a pub down the street from where I was staying and asked if he wanted to come. (Why not, right? I was in foreign territory.) He paused and then agreed with what seemed like not much enthusiasm. Though I could tell there was curiosity in his tone of voice.

What I didn't know was that after their soccer game, he and the entire team had been at a pub and I was a main topic of conversation—me and my "interesting" approach. Was it a dare? Why them? Apparently I had ridden my bike smack into a bunch of philosophers and physicists who studied at the prestigious Imperial College London. Hot *and* smart? Jackpot!

After Irish hung up with me, he proceeded to call every single dude on the team and every one of them showed up. I couldn't believe it. From that day on, Irish, Chris Sims, Richie, Elliot, and the rest of the Imperial College gang became great friends of mine. During my time there, I went to Stonehenge to visit Chris's family and traveled to Rhyl, Wales, to visit Elliot's family. These were the kinds of experiences I had dreamed of having when I originally considered living in another country. I now had my buds.

Do Cool Shit Takeaway

- Never be afraid to stray from the pack if you see an opportunity for a new experience.
- Fake it till you make it. Feeling insecure in a new setting is natural, but it can stop you from making a group of amazing new friends. Just go for it. People will generally be thrilled to meet a new person.
- No regrets! Imagine looking back on your life years from now. You want to be proud of your ability to embrace new opportunities.

Do Cool Shit Challenge

Meet a group of complete strangers on your own

Step 1: Wear a cool, eye-catching outfit.

Not to be superficial, but would you be more receptive to someone in an oversize, unflattering T-shirt and baggy jeans or someone in a really stylin' outfit? Plus, it may offer a topic for conversation! Go to urbanoutfitters.com or vogue.com to find out what's in season and add a personal twist to it. Or go to thrift stores and find clothes that match the current style if you can't afford to get things new. Thrift stores will never go out of style.

Step 2: Always approach people with a *big* smile!

It sounds so cheesy but it's *so* important! If you're frowning or neutral, people will mirror your expression, but if you go into a conversation with a big ole smile on your face and a twinkle in your eye, people will smile back and will respond to your positive energy. It disarms people and warms them up. If you need a second (and timeless) opinion, read Dale Carnegie's legendary book *How to Win Friends and Influence People*. It has a whole chapter about why smiling is so important.

Step 3: Think of some questions or icebreakers to kick-start a conversation.

A good trick is to ask people for advice. It gives people the opportunity to be an expert and take you under their wing. One example: "Hey! I'm new to the area and trying to figure out what's fun to do in this town. Got any ideas? I've gotten some bad ones so far, and you guys seem like you probably know where to go." Then smile again. (Compliments just don't get old.) Or go in with a funny joke to cut the tension of the room. My personal favorite:

Q: What does an angry pepper do?
A: It gets jalapeño face. [It gets all-up-in-yo face.]

Run this experiment and post your experience on docoolshit .org. I'd love to hear your stories!

OK, back to my British adventure.

Though my social life in London was going fantastically, the PR firm where I was interning was turning out to be the opposite. I spent all my days stuffing envelopes, making copies, and getting coffee for bosses who were bitchy, boring, and worse, had no interest in teaching me the business at all.

Now, I understood what an internship is. It's rarely a perfect experience, yet important to get your foot in the door of an industry that interests you, and for you to learn a bit about the day-to-day business in order to evaluate whether it's a potential career for you. But this was bad. For a month, I really tried to add value to their business. I let them know that I was willing to do other tasks and was ready to take on more responsibility. I tried to offer fresh ideas and ask smart questions, but they just wanted me to do my job and not make waves. Don't get me wrong, I was all about working my way up and starting from the bottom, but I couldn't do it without the respect of any of the people in the company and the knowledge that more learning was to come.

I could read the writing on the wall. I realized that this adventure in Europe was becoming a rote mind-numbing job and that I had more to offer. The thought of doing this for five more months was impossible. I decided that it was up to me to make the most out of my limited time in London and knew what I had to do.

Do Cool Shit Takeaway

It was in London that semester that I discovered the importance of the *MB* experience: the *mutually beneficial* experience.

Everything in life and business needs to be MB. When you buy something, it needs to be MB for the buyer and seller. When you build relationships with friends and colleagues, they need to be MB for both parties. If you're working for free as an intern, you need to get something out of it. When you think about the companies that succeed right now, they are MB companies.

Please ask yourself these questions:

- Is your current work/friend/romantic situation an MB experience?
- If it's not an MB experience, don't assume that your friend/teacher/boss is reading your mind. Have you *asked* for more responsibility/time/etc.?
- If you've done everything you can yet see the writing on the wall, is it time for you to start creating a better situation for yourself?

In order to do cool shit, all experiences and relationships must be mutually beneficial. Of course, you must "put in your time," but there must always be something to look forward to!

As for my hellish internship, I was not having any of it. I walked up to the head of the team, thanked her for the opportunity, and told her that I would not be interning for the company anymore.

I knew that there were serious consequences for quitting an internship, including the possibility of being sent home. So far, no student in the history of the Boston University internship program had ever quit a job. I would be the first one to stray.

I then went to the head of the internship program, Ranald Macdonald (not kidding, that's his name) and explained to him why I was just miserable at this internship and that I couldn't go back. He matter-of-factly explained to me that I might be sent home the next day, and I told him I understood. I spent one long night with my new British friends, explaining that it might be my last night there.

The next day Mr. Macdonald called me into his office.

"You know, there *is* a Lord in the House of the Lords looking for someone to help him with his British curriculum. Would you be interested in working with him? He is not often available, so you will have to do a lot of work alone."

Lord? British curriculum? Work on my own? Yes, please!

I accepted right away and proceeded to spend the next five months working for Lord Hugh Thomas, creating a visual-art project for him that described the history of England so he could use it in the classes he taught to foreign students. I got to do this on my own time. I could wake up when I wanted, set my own schedule, and mostly just work for myself. I had deadlines to meet but that was about it. It was my first taste of entrepreneurship, working independently, and motivating myself on my own. I loved working in this way, and in the end, the internship allowed me to travel, create a meaningful project, and deepen my friendships.

This experience made me realize how important it is to trust your gut, eliminate toxic situations, and surround yourself with positive, hard-working, inspiring people, which will inevitably make you want to elevate yourself as well.

With that in mind, here is a system I call **BET (bullet, eliminate, take on)** to help you stray from the group and get the results you want.

STEP 1: Create a bulleted list of commitments, affiliations, relationships, and individuals —those who *inspire* you on one side and those who *deplete* you on the other.

When I say *inspire*, I mean people who love life, who have the confidence you've always wanted, who have relationships that you admire, people you admire for their compassion or abilities, who are achieving amazing things in their life, and people who really support and care about you.

When I speak of people or relationships that *deplete*, I mean people who make you feel bad about yourself, or those who have a negative attitude, or who make you feel insecure, guilty, unsuccessful, or deflated.

I took a hard look at my friends at age twenty-five, and I discovered that there was a clear line between the people who made me feel good and those who made me feel bad. I wrote out the list of good and bad relationships and chose to reinvest my energy where it would be the most rewarding.

Keep in mind, some of the people on these lists may be popular in your friend circle, but let's be honest—sometimes bitches *are* popular. Really examine the nature of the relationship and if the negatives outweigh the positives, write that person's name down under your "deplete" list.

It's also OK if, once you write your list, you don't have a lot of people in the "inspire" column. I've had to start over a few times with only a few people who I could truly count on, and having a few true and loyal friends is better than a bunch of negative acquaintances any day.

It's important to take time every so often and think about your relationships. The people who bring positivity to your life are the ones you should choose to invest your energy in.

STEP 2: Eliminate the bad relationships and nurture the good ones.

All right. Now draw a big *X* through the people on the "deplete" list.

I don't mean to be simplistic. I know it can be complicated. But I also know that if you allow yourself to live or work with someone who makes you feel bad, it will hold you back.

If it's a friend who you need to eliminate, it may not seem easy at first, but when you start to really examine the relationships, you will become aware of how you *feel* when you are spending time with them. If you feel bad every time you see them (or guilty or negative or exhausted afterward), it's time to step away. Begin to take steps to spend less and less time with them until you can phase them out entirely. And if it's really bad, and they're a consistent and significant negative influence on your life, find their contact info in your phone and just press DELETE.

Or maybe you cared for this person at one point but they changed. Maybe they're Jekyll and Hyde. At some point, after the "I didn't mean it" and "give me another chance," you'll say, "Enough is enough."

In those moments, *deplete* equals *delete*.

This may sound really harsh. And you may be thinking, "It's a lot more complicated than this." The person who makes you feel bad could be a business partner or a boss. It could be a spouse.

Just think about it. Maybe you already tried being nice, attempting to reason with them in the past, but it backfired on you. Maybe you had a conflict that really never got resolved and you can tell that there were grudges still being kept. Or maybe, no matter how hard you tried to communicate, you just can't see eye to eye.

I had a friend from college who would almost always put me down when something good happened to me. If I met a new guy, she'd point out every one of his faults. If I got a really cool summer job, it was "luck." It took me a long time to realize that she wasn't my friend at all; she was just someone who was around and who had somehow become a consistent part of my life even though I didn't want her to be.

Don't worry about it. You'll see that with each person on the "deplete" list who you eliminate, you'll feel lighter and have more space to bring good into your life. Once you eliminate negative people from your life, it will free you up to devote more time and energy to cultivate the great friendships and relationships you have or want. You only have a limited amount of time to devote to your friends, so pick them wisely.

My kick-ass friend Marie Forleo has a saying that I firmly believe in: "Everything is figure-out-able." I promise your life will be so much better without the constant negative energy, and you will find love, a better-suited business partner, employees, and much better friends.

In the end, you'll wonder why it took you this long. Every time you make a decision on eliminating a toxic relationship in your life, you *will* get stronger and you'll have so much space for good shit to happen.

STEP 3: Take on new activities and relationships that are in line with what *you* want to be doing and that energize you.

Physically go to a place where people are doing the things you love and excel at or want to excel at. If you want to start a business in technology, you could go to a place like General Assembly (a start-up incubator) or WeWork Labs and connect with people there. Bring a friend the first time if you're intimidated. If you want to create a design product, find out when design meet-ups are happening on Meetup.com. Another great way to meet new people is through offering your services for free as an intern. More often than not, if you're friendly and sincere, you will start making great connections very quickly.

If you are a small-business owner or are launching your own business, you can find allies through various entrepreneurship groups in your city. You can contact your local chamber of commerce and join their small-business administration. Go to the businesses where you see good people working and ask them where they found their workers and if they know of other good people who are looking for jobs. Put feelers out on Facebook and Twitter.

This BET System will remove undue stress from your life, give you more time to find and do what *you* love, provide more time to build your business, and put a bounce back in your step. Straying from the group is the way to have the most unique opportunities to make new friends and build key contacts quickly in a new city. Being a sheep in the herd is not where you want to be, and you are only your best when you are surrounded by positive influences.

Take a BET on yourself. . . . Stray from the group.

3

HOW 9/11 CHANGED MY WORLD

What Is the Pivotal Moment That Will
Drive Change in You?

*Most people can look back over the years and identify a time
and place at which their lives changed significantly.*
—FREDERICK F. FLACK

I woke up, eyes still half-shut and bleary from the night before. I rarely drank too much, but somehow some college buddies whom I hadn't seen in a really long time convinced me to have "a couple more drinks" when we'd gone out the night before, which pretty much put me over the edge.

And boy did I pay for it the next morning. My head was pounding. Owie. As my eyes focused, I glanced at the alarm clock. And then did a double take. *What??* Ten o'clock?? How did that happen? How did I sleep through my alarm clock? That *never* happened to me! Adrenaline pumping through my veins, I shot out of bed, freaking out at the thought of being late for my job as an investment banker on Wall Street. I had been there only a few months, and it would *not* look good.

The first thing I did was call a car service, but a strange thing happened. The line was busy. Shit! I dialed again. Busy again! This car service was never this busy, especially at 10:00 a.m. on a weekday. What was going on? I called and called until finally someone picked up.

I shrieked, "I need a car in five minutes to Two World Trade Center, ASAP. I'm late for work!"

All I heard on the other end was a quiet voice. "Turn your TV on," he said.

I was like, "What? Turn my TV on? I am late for my job! I need a car now!"

Then all I heard again was "Turn your TV on." And then the voice on the other line hung up. What the F was going on? That was the most bizarre conversation I had ever had. So I did what I was told: I turned the TV on.

It was Tuesday, September 11, all hell had broken loose, and I watched in horror as the news showed clips of the twin towers going down. Of course, that was one of those days where everyone remembers exactly where they were and what they were doing. Everything froze. The world watched.

At the time, I was fresh out of college, having just finished twelve weeks of rigorous training in corporate finance and was three months into my crazy, nonstop job at Deutsche Bank, which was located directly across the street from the World Trade Center towers.

Most mornings at eight thirty, I would get off the subway under 2 World Trade Center and meet my college friend Laura for breakfast in the WTC courtyard. Laura worked for Aon, which occupied some of the highest floors of the tower. After breakfast, I would walk across the street to my office and begin my long day of looking through spreadsheets and financial models, all the while dreaming of playing soccer and my other secret passion: making movies.

I was supposed to be at the World Trade Center at the time the towers were hit, but I had happened to sleep through my alarm clock for the first time in my life.

As I watched my TV that morning, I felt helpless. I could do nothing but watch. My phone rang. It was my college boyfriend Zach, who somehow managed to get through to my cell phone to check to make sure I was okay. I had dozens of e-mails from family and friends asking me if I was safe, and one by one, in a daze, I wrote them all back that I was okay.

I found out later that two people in my office had died. Everyone else had run for cover and dove under cars and various structures seconds before thousands of pounds of shrapnel smashed down on the ground. My friend Laura lost more than four hundred of her Aon colleagues. (She went to get coffee when the plane hit her floor, which I only found out two weeks later—I thought she was dead, too.) It was just unbelievable.

I soon found out that all investment banks had "disaster recovery sites," which were massive warehouses (think boiler rooms) in the middle of nowhere (Piscataway, New Jersey) where the banks scrambled to get rows of desks together with computers and phones in place. We had to spend three and a half hours commuting each way (with rush hour traffic) to get to the disaster recovery site. We all did the best we could to adjust under the harsh circumstances.

A couple of months later, we got word that parts of the Deutsche Bank office building were safe enough to allow one person per group, accompanied by a trained marine, to retrieve critical, irreplaceable documents. I remember my heart racing when our CEO told us about this. I hadn't been there that day and felt so helpless. I really wanted to do something to help. I wanted to be the person to go in with the marine and retrieve the documents for the group and play a part, however small, in the recovery process.

As it turned out, I was the only one who volunteered to go, possibly because for those who were there on that day, going back in would have been too traumatizing. It was completely understandable.

I went through rigorous physical fitness tests (running a treadmill, breathing into contraptions, etc.), asbestos training (basically a lesson in what asbestos is and how to keep safe from it, as asbestos was a problem in those old buildings), mask-fitting class, and basic physical skills training to make sure I would not be a liability for the company. In the meantime, the bankers in my group put together pages and pages of things for me to retrieve. It was to be an incredibly challenging treasure hunt.

The day finally came. I was more ready than ever to go.

I met a marine at the base of the WTC site where they had set up a temporary headquarters. He handed me a moon suit, which covered my entire body except for my eyes, nose, and mouth, and gave me a gas mask and goggles for my face. I certainly felt like I could have been going to the moon. He handed me a flashlight and off we went.

When we walked into the Deutsche Bank building, I gasped. Where the beautiful fountain and golden escalator stood, it was now a pile of rubble. I'd never seen mounds of concrete and a building in pieces like this before. We climbed up the side stairs and walked toward the former elevator bank area, which used to be all shiny gold and was now covered with three inches of white powder.

We finally got to the floor where I used to work. My heart started to race.

It was bizarre. There were cups of coffee still sitting on tables. White soot covered everything. Some of the cubicles, including my own, were overturned. The marine and I heaved the edge of my cubicle wall just enough to expose some of my belongings. There was even an envelope with my mother's handwriting on it—she had sent a letter to my office congratulating me on my new job with some flowers.

I felt tears forming in my eyes. I grabbed the letter from my mom, tucked it away in my moon suit, and spent the next four hours hauling ten massive garbage bags full of items one by one from the elevator bank.

By this time, the marine and I had become buddies, and he even let me go to the "unsafe side" of the building, where the WTC debris had fallen through most of the side of our building. That was straight out of a movie. The windows were blown inward, glass was everywhere, every cubicle was smashed down, with papers and white powder everywhere, it was hard to imagine this place as a working investment bank just eight weeks prior.

One of the items not on the list that I found was our vice president's bicycle. I knew he loved that bike, so I brought that out as well. When I returned the bags of stuff to the team, our VP surprised me by letting me keep what turned out to be a very expensive bike, since he had already replaced it.

This was when I had my epiphany—my so-called aha moment.

I realized that so many people that day lost their lives and were unable to fulfill their dreams or find their true passions. Fortune gave me a chance to pursue mine. I knew I didn't want to squander this chance by continuing to work at a job I didn't love.

So I sold the bike, used the money to buy a new laptop, and began to write my first screenplay, since I'd wanted to do something creative as a career for a very long time.

A new chapter in my life was about to begin.

I'd like to challenge you by asking you two questions:

1. **What *thing* are you suppressing and/or looking for?**
2. **What type of excuses/fears/the unknown are holding you back?**

I created a simple two-step system that helped me change my reality:

STEP 1: Share your goal/dream/passion.

Take that thing that you want to do and start telling your closest friends about it. Tell the people who support you. It could be anything from losing weight to finishing your dream project that you started but got held up by a massive list of day-to-day unimportant tasks. It could be launching that great business idea that's been percolating in your mind for a long time or taking up that guitar lesson you always wanted to.

The first thing is to figure that *thing* out and start telling your supporters that you want to do it. By telling your friends about it, you are making an announcement to the people who you care about the most and they will support you through it and hold you accountable.

Let peer pressure work for you positively.

STEP 2: Next, once you have people cheering you on, create a **3-W Plan (What? Who? When?)**

WHAT *thing* are you trying to really accomplish? WHO are you approaching to help you accomplish your *thing*? Raise your hand and ask for what you want. WHEN is the deadline to finally make this happen?

Give yourself short deadlines. The longer your deadlines are, the less likely you will complete them. Create a basic schedule for yourself. Set weekly goals and mark them on your calendar and make yourself believe that if you don't meet your deadlines, you are fired from life. Be disciplined. What's the point in half-assing what you actually want to do in life?

The world can be molded to anything you want it to be. Start creating the best version of your own story and life by taking the steps now and not later.

4

MAKING THE TEAM

How to Go for It When You Think You Can't

*In order to succeed, your desire for success should be greater
than your fear of failure.*

—Bill Cosby

I waited with bated breath for the coach of the New York Magic to call
out the starting lineup.

This was the biggest moment of my career as a soccer player. It was
bigger than when I was four years old and scored my very first goal ever,
or when I made it to the national championships as a teenager. Here I
was, up against a hundred of the top college athletes, and I had already
dug so deep to make it there. I knew that if I made it on the starting
lineup of this team, then it would all have been worth it.

First, let me rewind a few months.

September 11 and the days that followed were the motivation I needed to realize that life can be so short and that I needed to start living the life I wanted to live now. The first thing I did was make a list of the big life goals I had for myself. It looked something like this:

- Play soccer professionally.
- Make movies.
- Start a business.

Short. Simple. To the point. Each of the items on this list was a dream I'd had for a while. At the time, I was still working at my investment banking job, but I decided that it was time to set about accomplishing the first goal on my list.

Soccer was first up for one reason. It's an incredibly physically demanding sport, and I knew I'd have a better shot at playing professionally while I was younger and more physically fit. As much as we'd like to, we can't ignore biology!

In college, I'd won Rookie of the Week when I scored two goals and had two assists in my first game ever as a Division I college player. (Radha wants you all to know that she assisted both of my goals.) I had started every game and was named All-League twice. But regardless of my strong college stats, the competition at this next level was way more hard-core.

I did some digging, looking into the New York women's soccer leagues. The New York Power was the main professional soccer club, but unless you played for a winning college program (Cornell's record was never fantastic, though we were a Division I school), it was hard to even get a tryout with them.

There was another route I could take. It was the Women's United Soccer Association (WUSA). This was the equivalent to the minor leagues, from which the pro teams look to pick their players. This was called the semiprofessional league, where players were given equipment, travel fare, food, trainers, physical therapists, everything a player needed—except a salary. I decided that it would be totally worth it for me to get a part-time job (maybe in the film business—goal number two!), and play soccer semiprofessionally until I could move up the ranks and score a tryout with the Power. I would get paid peanuts, but it would be enough to live on and, most important, I'd get to do what I loved every day. I even dreamed of a Nike sponsorship. You have to dream big! OK, OK, that was Step 5; I was getting ahead of myself.

Step 1 was to make a team.

I didn't know exactly how it would all go down, until I found out that the New York Magic were holding tryouts in Brooklyn. Step 1 was a go.

Unlike with the Power, any female player could try out, and the process would take two months, during which time the coaches would eliminate players at every practice and make their selection of eighteen players at the end, right before the season began. There would be scrimmages, real games, timed runs, and every ounce of our strength, stamina, and willpower would be tested.

The tryouts were held on Tuesday and Thursday nights from six to nine. Uh-oh. My first major hurdle: How on earth was I going to leave my banking job early enough to make it to tryouts twice a week? This meant that I would have to leave my office in Midtown at 5:00 p.m. at the absolute latest to barely get to tryouts on time—forget all about stretching, warming up, and mentally preparing myself. I was going to be up against the toughest competition of my life and definitely needed time to switch from "banker head" to "soccer superstar head."

Investment banking analysts work an average of ninety to one hundred hours per week, which amounted to about five dollars an hour when I did the math (best not to do the math—too depressing). It was meant to be one of the most prestigious jobs you could get right out of college, but long hours in the office were the norm and the bank owned your life. It was basically a sweatshop for naive college graduates.

I checked Google Maps and it said that it would take one and a half hours via subway or about fifty minutes via car (without traffic) from Midtown. I didn't have a car. I was screwed.

But then it hit me.

The car service guys downstairs! They were my buddies. One of the perks of working for an investment bank was having free car service late at night so you can be driven home and not have to pay for a taxi or take the subway at 3:00 a.m. I had already befriended all of the car service guys because they were *real* salt-of-the-earth people, unlike some of the stuffier banker types. I snuck them food from time to time and always spent a few minutes shooting the breeze with them. We shared some laughs together and really connected as friends.

The same day I found out about the tryouts, I set the wheels in motion.

It was this opportunity that taught me how to *just ask* for something that is meaningful and important to me. It was this experience that taught me the power of empathy.

I approached my favorite driver, Ahmed, and told him all about my dream to play soccer professionally. He was from the Middle East, where soccer is hugely popular, so he got it. I then told him about my plan and how he could help. You'll find that most people will do what they can to help others fulfill their dreams; it's a powerful feeling. He loved the idea of my being able to try out for a semiprofessional team and agreed to drive me.

I then went to my other boys, the security guards Jamaal and Steve. I told them about my plan and asked them if they'd be willing to store my soccer bag behind their desk and bring it outside and give it to Ahmed at 4:30 p.m. The security guards were not allowed to store anything behind the desks, but they could tell how much this all meant to me and agreed.

All I needed to do now was to find an ally in my group at the bank who understood why this dream was so important. I knew just the guy—the managing director, Bill, whom I became close with after 9/11 (he and his family had actually put me up in their house for a week or so after the attacks since it became too hard to commute across the Brooklyn Bridge). He was the one who I knew would empathize with me *and* had the power to actually give me the permission to do this. He had played soccer in college—it was actually what we first connected about when I got to the bank—and this gave me the courage to *just ask* him for what I wanted.

I made sure to have a plan when I walked into his office. I needed to establish why this opportunity was meaningful to me and make sure to convey that I also understood my responsibilities at the bank.

"Hi, Bill, how are you?" I said.

"Good," he replied, still looking at his computer screen. "What's up?"

"Listen, I wanted to talk with you about something that really means a lot to me." He stopped reading his e-mail and focused on me.

"I have a once-in-a-lifetime opportunity to try out for the New York Magic, the WUSA soccer team. I know I can make this team if I put my mind to it, and I know you of all people can understand why this is such a special opportunity for me. I also understand that I have responsibilities here at the bank. The tryouts are twice a week from six to nine p.m. for the next two months, and I will come back to the office after the tryouts to finish whatever work I have left. I have enough energy to do both, and I am committed to making both work. I am asking for your permission, and if I make the team, I'd love for you and your daughter to come to a game! I can teach her a few tricks too!"

He really couldn't say no. I knew I had some serious work cut out for me, but I'd proved that I could be trusted to come back to the bank on those nights to finish the work that I missed. He knew I wouldn't let him down. A good boss will understand the importance of going after your dreams, even if it may mean no longer working with them. Bill understood.

Do Cool Shit Takeaway

How to Ask for What You Want

If you need to escape your day job for a couple of hours per week to follow your passion project, approach the person you think would most likely say yes and be an ally for you. Find out beforehand what their hobbies are. Use that knowledge to connect with them about what you have in common. Also, prior to approaching them, make sure you have particularly excelled at work in the past several weeks and that they took notice. This will help so much when you make your request.

Step 1: Approach the kindest person in your company who is in a senior position, who you either directly report to or is a peer of someone you directly report to.

Wait for them to stop what they are doing and fully give you their attention. Don't continue speaking until they are completely focused on you since this may be your one shot to get them to say yes.

Step 2: Be specific with your question.

"This opportunity requires me leaving the office for x hours x times per week." You must be as specific as you can without compromising the opportunity. Say the number of days and the hours involved. The more specific you are, the more likely they can wrap their minds around it and agree to it.

Step 3: Establish that you have their back.

"I know my job is of utmost priority, so I will make sure that everything I need to do will be completed on time and I will work late and on weekends if need be in order to honor my commitment to this project."

Step 4: Ask for their blessing.

"I am asking for your blessing to help me fulfill a dream of mine." Place the person in your shoes, helping them share in the excitement you have for this particular plan. This would make it very hard for any boss to say no.

You have to follow through and do your work. If you don't follow through after the first couple of weeks, they will take this opportunity away from you. It's entirely up to you to go above and beyond at your job and make them happier and subsequently not care that you are leaving for a few hours here and there every week.

There is now a big trend in many businesses toward more flexible work hours. It may not work in banking (although it did for me!), but in many offices, flexible hours can be established. There is also a trend toward allowing more employees to work from home (it saves the company money if they're in a cramped office space). Whatever the dream is, finding out about your company's flexible work hours policy would be helpful in the "ask."

Also, be prepared to answer some hard questions.

In the event that your passion project may cause you to leave your day job, your employer may want to know if you are planning to leave. In this case, at first say, "This is a thing I *have* to try or I will forever regret it, and it has been a long-term goal of mine. I am, however, committed to this job too, so I plan to see it through at the same time." Don't worry them until you really have to give them notice.

After you spend a few weeks on your passion project and if you really want to move forward with it and leave your day job, walk into your boss's office and say: "Thank you so much for letting me discover what I'm truly passionate about. *You* helped *me*, and I want to help *you* find and train the new employee who will replace me." This way, you are really honoring your boss and they may be grateful that you are ending this relationship respectfully and seamlessly. Give them at least three weeks to find and train a replacement. Do a great job training your replacement, as it's important to maintain good relationships with former employers. You never know when you may need them again. Create a training manual for the person who is replacing you if one doesn't exist. Go above and beyond. It's good karma and will bless your next endeavor.

. . . .

Bill asked me that I keep my tryout plan on the down low, understandably, so I had to figure out how to escape the other investment banking analysts twice a week for two months. I started by putting some papers in a FedEx box and pretending like I was going to the mail room, and then I would walk outside, turn the corner, and jump in the car that was waiting for me with my soccer bag in the backseat. I had to change into my soccer gear, stretch, and mentally prepare in the car. I asked Ahmed to put a James Bond soundtrack in the CD player so that I could get pumped up on the way. I have to admit, I kind of felt like 007.

When I got to the fields on the first day, there were one hundred girls there, all suited up, with rolled-up ankle tape as headbands (hard-core soccer-chick style) and ready to go. I hadn't touched a ball in a couple of weeks and was worried I'd have trouble finding my confidence. I reminded myself that I was playing soccer by age three and scoring eleven goals in one game at age eleven and attending national championships by age fourteen. I belonged here. I grabbed a ball and started dribbling down the field, warming up. I was small compared to the other girls but knew my strengths and where I could beat the others. Still, I knew I had to figure out a way to stand out from the rest of the girls. I had to do something different.

The opportunity came when I spotted the head coach. I walked over to him, knowing that he's Italian, and said with a smile, "*Io mi chiamo Miki. Come ti chiami? Mi piacciono i ragazzi italiani.*" This translates to "My name is Miki. What's your name? I like Italian men." I travel a lot and basically learned how to say, "My name is Miki. What's your name?" and then some sort of pickup line in ten different languages throughout the years. That last line would always make a person laugh, which is such a great icebreaker. People often immediately open up if you can make them laugh.

Thankfully, the coach laughed, which gave me the opening to say something more. I quickly and passionately told him my story. I asked that he consider me as a strong right-midfield candidate. I told him I had the stamina to handle the entire outside corridor from one end of the field to the other, to both attack and defend, but that I was an even more deadly attacking midfielder. I had good speed and used my small size to my advantage by sneaking past the defense quickly. I wanted him to know that there were significant advantages to having a smaller player on the field. I mean, look at the Spanish national team play the German national team. The Germans are two heads taller, but the small Spaniards turn so much faster with the ball and can cut through opponents with much more ease.

I thanked him for the opportunity, and I ran off to join the others and made sure to do some dribbling moves with the ball while he was watching. I absolutely *had* to separate myself from the crowd and get noticed immediately. It didn't have to be obnoxious; I just had to find the right opportunity when nobody was around so I could plant a seed.

When he blew his whistle, we all headed out onto the field.

He immediately called my name because he remembered me from earlier and placed me on the first team. I was *so* glad I made the move to talk to him (and tell him that I liked Italian men!).

The scrimmages went really well. I played my heart out, assisted a few goals, and scored one of my own. At the end of the tryout, the coach called my name back for the next tryout. I had made round two!

I made it through second round and then the third round and amazingly the fourth! And every round until the end of the two months. The day finally came when I got the call from the head coach himself. With a thick Italian accent, he said, "Miki, you made it. Congratulations."

I couldn't believe it. I had made it! Step 1: accomplished. It felt amazing. I called Ahmed and told him first. He was the one who had sat patiently and waited for three hours for the tryouts to be completed and he was the one who drove me back to the bank every night after the tryouts were over at nine. He was overjoyed. Needless to say, I celebrated with the security guards. I had done all this and kept my promise to Bill. I had worked after every tryout until two or three in the morning and had gotten everything I needed to get done at the bank.

But now what? I had made the team. Do I quit my banking job now?

I decided to play my first game with the Magic before doing anything drastic just to see how it would go down. Maybe I would ride the bench the whole game and it would suck.

But when the day came to announce the starting lineup, they called my name. It was incredible. I had. Made. The. Starting. Lineup. Tears welled up in my eyes, but I wiped them away and quickly jumped to my feet to put on my socks and cleats. There's no crying in soccer!

The team suited up and headed onto the field, my heart pounding so quickly as adrenaline rushed through my veins. The referee whistled and the game began. We had won the kickoff, so our striker handed the ball to the center mid, who handed it to me. I dribbled down the right, juked the right defender, and crossed the ball to our striker. Two things happened almost immediately. Our striker connected with the ball and we scored, and the defender came straight at me and slid into my leg as my foot was planted firmly in the grass.

My sheer joy at assisting the goal was shattered immediately. You could hear the snap from across the field. It was the tell-tale sound of a torn ACL, the anterior cruciate ligament in the knee that holds everything together. I crumpled to the ground in agony, crying and clutching my left leg.

After such a long fight to get to this point and after all that I had gone through, to then have my season end within the first five minutes of my first game of my professional career was nothing short of *devastating*. I knew that this would be a long road to recovery. I had never worked so hard in my entire life to reach a goal, and to see it taken away so quickly? Unbelievable.

I was carried off the field with the crowd clapping in support and that was it. At that moment, I was so glad I hadn't quit my job at the bank because I needed the very best health insurance to cover my knee surgery and get sports therapists to nurse me back to health.

I went back to my bank the next Monday, on crutches, and tearfully told Bill what happened. He felt my pain and gave me two weeks' leave of absence after my surgery so I could recover and regain strength.

The surgery was shockingly painful. The physical therapy was too. It was a full eight months before I was able to play soccer again. But I made it through, went to sports therapy diligently three times per week, and came back stronger than ever. I was still working at the bank while recovering, and I was so ready to try out again.

And I did. I did it all over again. And I made the starting lineup of the New York Magic all over again. I played a strong season but, un-believably, in a semifinal game, I was tackled again when my *other* foot was planted and I tore my *other* ACL, in my right knee. Tearing both of the major ligaments in my knees, two seasons in a row? Are you bloody *kidding* me? I could feel the pain from the surgery and weeks of waking up in the middle of the night in absolute agony. I could hear the physical therapist cranking at my knee to bend because it wouldn't, with tears of pain streaming down my face and my jaw clenched as tight as it could. I could feel my armpits hurting from the constant crutching around everywhere.

I knew that this was it for me and my dream to play soccer profes-sionally. My body was saying *no*. I could have come back again, but I knew that if another major knee injury happened, I'd be getting my knees replaced before age forty.

As I was carried off the field for the second time within the year, I paused to reflect on what had become a soccer career cut short. My mind went back to when I was three and kicked a ball for the first time while wearing a dress, and then fast-forwarded all the way up to this final moment, twenty-one years later. I could remember all of the home and away games with the various teams I played on, the countless weekends I sacrificed for this sport, the celebratory team dinners, the pep talks, the toughest losses, and the most unexpected victories. I'd formed incredibly close bonds with not only the team players but also all of the families who traveled together and got to know one another. I was always so aware of the sacrifices our parents made for us to pursue this sport to such a level. Soccer truly was one of the biggest parts of my life thus far, and some of the best and toughest lessons I ever learned were thanks to this dear sport. Ultimately, while I was saying good-bye to soccer, I felt satisfied because I knew I had given it my all—my absolute all. Sometimes, life throws us curve balls when we least expect it, just to see how we handle it and also to point us in the direction that we're meant to go in.

I took a deep breath, looked back at the field with love in my heart, and closed my eyes for a moment. I knew that at the close of this chapter, new and great adventures would be right around the corner.

Do Cool Shit Takeaway

- Even if you think something seems impossible at first, figure out how to make it work. You have to show tenacity and go for it!
- Just ask for what you want. You may be surprised at how things always seem to work out.
- Establish why your goal is meaningful or important to you. If you need something from a boss or friend, show them your passion and connect with them about their own passions. They will more than likely empathize with your situation and do what they can to help you out.
- Make sure you follow through on your promises.
- Separate yourself from your competition. Transform seemingly negative situations into positive ones.
- Life throws unexpected curve balls that don't always go your way and may be out of your control. Move on quickly, dwelling on it serves no benefit to you or anyone around you. Focus on new dreams.
- Make 'em laugh!

Whenever you feel like something is impossible and that there is no *way* you can do something like leave your grueling day job to follow your passion project, ask yourself this first:

What would MacGyver do?

You know how MacGyver used to get himself into sticky situations, then get out of them by constructing a bomb made out of chewing gum and packing tape? Use MacGyver as your inspiration for real-life problems. Step outside your situation and imagine what (seemingly crazy) ways you can come up with to solve your problem. Maybe the first couple of ideas you have won't work, but my bet is you'll stumble across a workable solution using this method.

The overall idea here is for you to get your hands dirty in your passion project to see if it's something you're willing to go all in on (quit your day job!) or if it's not something that is the right fit after all. It's so good to mitigate some of the risk by keeping your day job at first and seeing if this new opportunity makes sense for you. Many times, when you dig into the nuts and bolts of any passion project, you will see that all businesses have paperwork, busy work, challenges, and frustrations.

No matter what, working on something you are passionate about always trumps any day job to solely make money. If you're going to deal with any of those pesky issues I mentioned, you may as well do them for yourself, and not for someone else—*and* for something you are truly passionate about.

5

FINDING YOUR CALLING

How to Ask Yourself the Right Questions

I've come to believe that each of us has a personal calling
that's as unique as a fingerprint.

—OPRAH WINFREY

A frantic voice shouted at me as I put the phone to my ear.

"Miki! He wants Wall Street to be closed in two days! Completely closed! I need you to make it happen!"

Then the phone went dead.

He needed Wall Street closed in two days? Seriously? I had been on the job for a total of two months and had no idea if this was even in the realm of possibility. How on earth was I going to pull *this* off?

So . . . **after my** soccer career came to a screeching halt and I left my investment banking job after I made the team the second time, I decided that rather than jumping right into the next thing like an excited puppy, I had to pause and contemplate my next move. I had spent two years working one hundred hours a week on Wall Street and was completely burned-out. This was the perfect time to employ what I call the **I-EX— internal examination.**

I knew that if I just went for the next thing that came my way, I might be headed for another burnout in a year or two. Burnouts are cool (and impressive) once. (Don't most superstars go through a sexy burnout phase?) Twice, not so much.

This I-EX would be my North Star, the little arrow on the compass that would point me in the right direction. And I desperately needed it.

It began with asking myself two key questions:

1. **What am I *really* good at?**
2. **What am I passionate about?**

QUESTION 1: WHAT AM I *REALLY* GOOD AT?

This question reminds me of a story that my dad told me when I was a young girl. When he was just a kid in India, he loved Bollywood movies and decided that he wanted to be a singer. So he went to a famous Indian music teacher to audition. My dad sang his innocent little heart out, and once he finished his song, the teacher paused and said to him: "How about tabla?" (Tabla is the hand drum.) My dad learned early on that he did not have the gift of song (truly, he was and still is tone-deaf—love you, Pops!) so he pursued what came more naturally to nerdy Indians like him and the other thing that he was passionate about: engineering.

The lesson I took from this story was to try to surround myself with people honest enough to prevent me from making a total fool out of myself.

I was no Adele, but I definitely had a few things to offer.

I wrote down a list of my top skills—the ones about which I'd received positive feedback.

Honest external feedback is critical in understanding if you're actually *good* at something. Someone should have given Vanilla Ice some honest external feedback a long time ago and saved us all from his transgressions.

I've broken it down into two skill categories: personal and professional.

Personal: Sports, fitness, communicating with people, traveling with ease (because I speak multiple languages), making friends quickly, writing

Professional: Marketing, business development, writing, organizing, languages

At twenty-four years old, this was all that I knew about myself.

QUESTION 2: WHAT AM I PASSIONATE ABOUT?

Here's where my dreams list came in. I wanted to play soccer professionally (unfortunately, I ended up crossing that one off all too expeditiously), make movies, and start a business. This was the fun part—I let my imagination go and allowed myself to dream.

I caught the movie bug early on, as my mother was a total movie buff with a special love for the older black-and-white movies with stars like James Dean and Clark Gable (dreamy!). I never really wanted to be on-screen but I really liked the idea of being behind the scenes—particularly screenwriting and production. I just loved the creative process of filmmaking.

While in college, I had spent the summers after my sophomore and junior years interning in Los Angeles. Cornell had a relationship with some film production companies in Los Angeles, and through our university career center Rads and I both scored the same internship at a film studio, where we spent two summers reading screenplays and living the dream in California. I was comfortable in the creative setting, and I worked hard to give precise and constructive feedback for each screenplay I read. The producers gave me great feedback for my work and handed me positive recommendation letters when the internship was completed.

So here I had a dream that I was passionate about—storytelling through film—and I had the positive feedback that showed me I *did* have some of the skills necessary to be an asset to this industry. Time to get on it!

Rads helped me get an interview with a film production company that worked mainly on television commercials. At this point, she was a full-fledged commercial agent for big directors like George Lucas, Robert Altman, and Zack Snyder.

During my interview at the production company for the associate producer position, I told James, the owner of the company, that I knew quite a bit about finance (I knew enough from the banking days) and so I painted a visual picture of how I could help take his company to the next level by introducing him to producers and agents I had met in Los Angeles during the two summers I was there. I also told him that my twin sister was a commercial agent and she knew a lot of people in advertising who could potentially get us more shoots to produce. I used the words *we* and *us* a lot so that he could visualize us working together. I said things like, "When we approach new clients, I think a creative way for us to do it would be . . ." Subtly, I spoke as though I were already hired.

I showed lots of passion for the film business and told him about the two college summers I spent in Los Angeles reading scripts. I made sure that he knew that I went to Cornell. I was still paying off my never-ending student loans, so I brought up my degree at every opportunity, otherwise what was even the point of getting the degree? Thankfully, he was sufficiently impressed and gave me the gig.

My associate producer job consisted mainly of project managing the various commercial and music video shoots that were happening at the production company, sometimes with big stars like Beyoncé and Mary J. Blige. I had to help hire the freelance production team to work on the shoots. Once the freelance production team was hired, they would then hire the rest of the crew, which included the key gaffer (lighting tech), the key grip (rigging tech), the DP (cinematographer), and the camera team. I also had to deal with location scouts and talent agents and help manage and pay invoices as they came in.

I really liked the project management part of the job, and I had a talent for getting things done quickly. I figured out that being efficient with my time was key. I organized the office in a way that I could pretty much reach everything I needed to within two or three feet from my desk chair. It saved so much time!

Putting out fires in the film business was super fun too. Once, James called me, frantic and stressed out because he was given a last-minute request by one of his prima donna directors for a shoot that was happening in two days' time.

The director requested for the shoot that we have:

- a live horse
- an English police officer uniform
- a red double-decker tour bus
- Wall Street completely closed off for the shoot

As I scanned the list, wondering how the hell I was going to get all of this stuff in twenty-four hours, my eyes hit the last item on the list. I'm sorry, *what*? I needed to completely close off Wall Street by tomorrow?

With no alternative, I decided the best way to handle this was to try to have fun and make it a personal challenge. Stressing wouldn't have helped anyway.

I managed to find an animal rental company fairly quickly and rented the horse. Then I called the uniform rental company and found the police uniform, contacted the tour bus company and gave them an opportunity to showcase their bus on a commercial for free (all we had to pay for was gas, so we ended up saving a ton of money). Next, I rushed to the mayor's office to see if I could get the permits needed to close off Wall Street for ten hours, in just one day. I sat there for the better part of the day, waiting for the permit office to see what they could do. In the meantime, I brought them all a fruit-and-cheese plate and made sure I made everyone in the office smile at least once. After many hours of waiting and smiling (my cheeks were hurting at this point), they finally managed to get us the permits (I think the fruit-and-cheese plate did a lot of the talking). Victory!

I had managed to pull all of this off, so *of course* at the last minute, the client decided that he didn't want to shoot on Wall Street and got another location secured on the morning of the shoot. And *of course* the client didn't want the horse either. Oh well. So it goes in the crazy production world. Being flexible was a fast lesson I learned that day.

At this point in my journey, I was only a couple of years out of college, and this situation was a wonderful reminder of two things:

1. **Anything is possible if you set your mind to it.**
2. **Freaking out never helps.**

Once things settled down a bit, I started studying the invoices that were being paid to the various departments and discovered that free-lancers got paid much more per day than I (and the other full-timers) did. Not only did they make much more per day, but they also didn't work every day (only when they were hired for shoots), meaning they had time to pursue other interests for the rest of the month if they wanted to. This was definitely appealing to me.

OK, yes, I also understood the big downside: freelancers never knew when their next job would come. I could get ten days of guaranteed work, followed by twenty days' worrying about where the next paycheck would come from.

I was surprisingly OK with that uncertainty. I knew that if I kicked ass on shoots as a freelance producer, I would be hired again. I just had to do a killer job.

This was going to be my first taste of entrepreneurship. It meant that

I had to hunt for gigs and offer a service that people wanted. And I had to be better than everyone else in order to be hired again.

I made the decision and quit working in-house and went freelance as soon as one producer agreed to hire me as a production assistant on the set of his next commercial. It was a step down on the professional ladder, but it was the only way to be on my own in the business. The production assistant did everything from renting vans to picking up props, driving around directors and clients, getting coffee for people, doing all the menial work on set like picking up trash, and anything that the production team needed.

You can imagine the call I had to make to my parents. Not only did I quit my cushy banking job, but I was quitting a job with security and *choosing* one where I pick up trash and get people coffee. My mother would have had a heart attack, so of course that's not how I explained it to them. I told them that I had an incredible opportunity to work on set and move up the ranks with an eye toward becoming a producer who makes $1,000 per day. It usually took about three to four years to get to producer status from production assistant, but I told my parents I was on a six-month fast track (a self-imposed track of course). It was the only way to get the blessing from my much more conservative-career-track-loving parents. With furrowed eyebrows, they gave their good wishes.

Once I got on set, I did everything I could to garner the attention of the producers and production managers while I was running around. My goal was to move up the ranks quickly and get a job as an office production assistant, which was one step up from set production assistant—this meant that I didn't have to pick up trash anymore and I would be only one producer's bitch instead of a whole group's (*woohoo!*). It meant that I would make copies, put production books together, and help hire the rest of the freelancers.

I knew that once I got into the production office as a freelancer, I'd be able to work my way up faster. I told the producer that I went to Cornell and that I was a former investment banker. This time, that didn't impress them *at all*. They looked at me with squinted eyes that clearly read "Who gives a shit?" What did impress them was getting shit done. And getting shit done right. And getting shit done fast. I learned this very quickly and just put my head down and worked my tail off. What I really liked about this kind of work was that it was never boring. Every day was different, every shoot was different, and every project had its own set of unique challenges. Very often I would ask myself the old "What would MacGyver do?" question, which on so many occasions would take me outside the pressure of the situation to come up with unique solutions—like the time I found a shoot location in the eleventh hour by convincing a perfect stranger to let us shoot in his home. It was those unique solutions that got the attention of the producers.

Thankfully, I moved up the ranks quickly, according to my plan. Within three months, I was production coordinating, and within six months, I was producing shoots. They were smaller shoots but it didn't take me long (the standard three years or so) to get to become a full producer.

When work was slow to come in, I spent my time building my Rolodex of potential clients. I stopped by all the local production companies and I figured out whom to talk to (usually the in-house producer), took them to lunch, and asked to be given the chance. I asked them to think about what it was like when they first got their big break. A little nostalgia goes a long way. I usually got the jobs when nobody else was available and they had exhausted all of their contacts (totally fine with me!). At least I was on their radar. This business is all about relationships, and I think they felt safer knowing that they had at least *met* me once, rather than picking a name out of the production guidebook at random.

Banging down doors of the production companies was a tremendous way of preparing myself for entrepreneurship—it gave me thick skin and along the way taught me how to mentally deal with rejection (something that felt like multiple punches to the kidneys at first). It also helped me think quickly on my feet if I was met with an angry secretary or gatekeeper. As you've seen in previous chapters, it turns out that bringing people free food is almost always a golden entry ticket. (At the core, we're all just animals aren't we?)

As I was producing commercials, I gained more and more understanding of this business and about project management.

Then something happened to me that changed the course of my life.

My true entrepreneurial journey was about to begin.

Do Cool Shit Exercise

These questions below may seem obvious to you but many people have a hard time being honest with themselves. This is another kick in the ass for you to actually do it properly.

What am I *really* good at?

You must be able to articulate in words why you are great. You must show external proof that others have said the same thing about you. There is no fooling yourself.

Within "What am I really good at?" answer the following:

(A) What are the biggest problems I've solved?

- Did you change an angry customer's mind about your product?
- Did you solve a defect in your offering?
- Did you streamline a process to make things more efficient?
- How did you show resourcefulness to solve a problem?

(B) What do I have to contribute to a team/workplace?

- Are you good at leading small groups?
- Are you generally a happy person, thus improving work environment?

- Have you done anything to improve company culture? Did you organize a memorable team outing? Did you get the people in your office together for something fun?
- Are you a self-starter?
- Can you get people to follow what you started?
- What's a time you managed exceptionally?

(C) What are the tangible skills I have that others don't?
- Do you excel at special computer programs, computer languages, or other creative skills?
- Do you speak any languages fluently?
- Are you a great photographer?
- Are you exceptional creatively?
- What do you do best in the opinion of your peers?

When you are in an interview, always give the interviewer a vision of tomorrow, the notion that with *your* help, you can take the company to the next level. Giving someone a mental picture of growing the business together (with you in it) and that you will add tangible value to the business beyond just the daily duties, is where the excitement comes from for any employer.

If you don't have any marketable skills, don't panic. Start by taking classes! You can take free design and Photoshop classes at the Apple store, you can pretty much get any tutorial now on YouTube.com, and you can also find *so* much information on Google. My close friend Manick went from being an investment banker to learning how to code on his own at a very high level in *less than three months* because he dedicated himself to it day in, day out, for three straight months. Now he is launching one of the smartest companies for music that exists online, Rukkus .com, a website for music lovers to discover new music and easily find out where the bands are playing. He built the entire back end of his website by himself. Three months of dedication, in the grand scheme of things, is nothing. Fully dedicating yourself to something for only a few months upfront can reap benefits for the rest of your life. By the way, for those of you excited about learning some code—a useful skill for pretty much any entrepreneur these days—you can also attend Codecademy (codecademy.com) to learn various computer programming languages quickly.

Once you figure out what you're good at, it's so much easier to ask yourself the next question:

What am I passionate about? What am I *really* good at? By now you know that you can pick your passion project only within the realm of the things you are *actually* good at. You must pick a passion project utilizing your talents, the things that your most trusted people around you say you're exceptional at! You can work in the music industry if you really like music, but you may not end up a singer.

Within "What am I passionate about?" answer the following:

(A) What do I like to do for fun?
- Do you like to build things for fun?
- Do you like to write for fun?
- Do you like to volunteer and work with kids?
- Do you like to cook?

(B) What's the last thing I've done that I'm proud of?
- Have you helped someone else achieve something?
- Have you built something that is important for the community?

- Have you supported a group or community through a rough period?

(C) Are there any communities, people, places, or issues that I care about supporting?

- Are you passionate about helping your family and friends?
- Are you passionate about storytelling?
- Are you passionate about human rights?
- Are you passionate about women's issues?

After you have identified what you are good at and then what you are passionate about, now it's time to apply it.

6

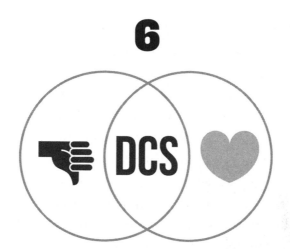

WHAT SUCKS IN YOUR WORLD

How to Put Your Passion in Motion

Status quos are made to be broken.

—RAY DAVIS

I clutched my stomach in pain for what seemed like the third time that week. After a long day of working on set of a Victoria's Secret commercial (yes, Adriana Lima is that hot), gastro pain was the last thing I wanted to deal with *again* when I got home. This time though, it was worse—a cross between serious bloating and sharp abdominal pain.

Why was this happening? I never had this kind of stomach pain before, but it now seemed to be a constant foe! I simply couldn't live this way.

What had I been eating? I knew I had been eating crappy, unhealthy, processed food on set of the commercials and I had ordered some creamy dish that night (man, it was good). I recall wolfing it down before speaking to anyone at dinner. I've always been a fast eater, since I grew up with an identical twin sister with an identical starvation syndrome (*and* with an older sister who was less than one year older than us). The three of us would race to the kitchen table and play a game of "How much food can I stuff inside myself before I can grab seconds?" It was tough competition. My poor parents were left with scraps.

Now, I really had to do something. There had already been too many times I'd pulled the old "it wasn't me" line when my stomach was upset. (You know that move, you've done it before, don't pretend.)

As I sat on my couch with a hot water bottle leaning against my belly to soothe it, I opened up my laptop and did what any modern-day human would do: I googled it.

It didn't take me long to figure out what was bothering my stomach. I self-diagnosed myself as lactose intolerant. In my research, I read that one in five Americans is lactose intolerant and that 80 percent of the world is lactose intolerant to varying degrees. Most humans lack the enzyme to break down lactose, which is present in all dairy products. The symptoms include bloating, stomach pain, and gas. Aha! I figured it out! That was easy.

I then decided I would conduct an experiment: I would not eat dairy for a month and see how I felt. Within a week, the bloating, stomach pain, and gas were gone. (See, Pops? Who needs medical school?) Very quickly though, I began to miss eating a lot of my favorite foods: ice cream, grilled cheese, and most important, pizza. It required every bit of self-restraint not to eat pizza, especially late at night. The scent of slices called to me from every corner of every block of New York City, and I had walk with my head down a lot.

A few weeks into my dairy experiment, I traveled to a small country town in the South of France. And when you're in France, you *have* to eat cheese. It's blasphemous if you don't. So I caved and I ate it—a lot of it (I did bring a whole container of Tums with me just in case), and then braced myself for what was to come . . .

And nothing did. Nothing happened. No bloating, no stomachache, and no pain.

Huh?

Why couldn't I eat dairy at home but could eat it in the French countryside? I asked the proprietors of the farm-style restaurants about the cheese I had eaten. They told me they made the milk right there in their backyard and made the cheese themselves. Interesting.

The reason my stomach was so happy in France was becoming clear to me. American dairy manufacturers were injecting tons of hormones into the cows so they can produce more milk, giving them antibiotics and feeding them pesticide-filled feed, all of which was affecting the dairy we ate and all of which gave us the stomachaches, bloating, and intolerance.

I started eating organic and humanely treated dairy to see if that would be OK for my stomach, and sure enough, it was! My stomach (also known as my petri dish) was able to stomach this *good* kind of dairy. I wondered if others knew this *before* they swore off their favorite foods, like pizza.

I started dreaming about pizza. I loved it! I loved what pizza stood for. It stood for inclusion of rich, poor, old, and young. It welcomed all ethnicities. It reminded me of my favorite childhood memories, so many random dates and late-night study sessions. Pizza was a true mash-up of cultures, we ate with our hands, and we laughed and cried with a great pizza pie. It was truly amore.

I then started researching to see if there were alternatives available. I didn't really find anything good. I did find one small hole-in-the-wall place in the East Village, but it didn't offer organic or local dairy. I discovered that pizza is a $32 billion industry, it accounts for 10 percent of American food service sales, and Americans, on average, eat one hundred *acres* of pizza every single day. Wow.

OK, if *I* gave up on pizza because it made my stomach hurt, and one in five Americans is intolerant to American dairy, so *they* gave up pizza too, it meant that 20 percent of Americans were in the same boat as me. If I missed pizza, then surely some of these 20 percent of the people missed pizza too!

There it was.

I needed to open up my own alternative pizzeria, using fresh, local, and organic ingredients, a place where everyone with any allergy can come and eat a wonderful slice of pizza. Gluten intolerant, dairy intolerant, wheat intolerant, whatever, it didn't matter, anyone would get to eat delicious pizza!

I daydreamed about having a cozy place where friends could meet. I wanted to work with local farms and serve drinks made locally. I wanted my pizza boxes to be made locally. I wanted to be an advocate for local farmers and businesses. I wanted it to be like that gem of a place I saw in the South of France where they milked their own cows and made their own cheese in their backyard. Although, given the price of real estate in Manhattan, maybe I'd nix the cow part.

This kind of pizza safe haven didn't exist anywhere in New York City at the time. I did my research. There were hundreds of pizza shops on every corner but nothing like the one that I was imagining. *But* I knew nothing about the restaurant business. I knew nothing about starting a business at all. Luckily, I had some extra time to learn more since I was still working as a freelance producer. In between shoots, I was able to further explore this new project.

There were three different routes I could take to get to my goal.

The first was the philanthropic route. I could become an advocate for local farms and local businesses and help them get off the ground and perhaps also see what they are up to and how they started their businesses.

The second was the intrapreneurial route. This meant that I could try and get a job with an existing pizza company or a restaurant group and try to show them why creating a healthy pizza side to their business would be an interesting opportunity. I could explain to them that Whole Foods was on the rise and that even Walmart was embracing organic produce (which was a clear sign that all of America was headed that way) and that their company needed to do the same. I could basically be an entrepreneur within an existing organization. I could come up with ideas and help the company put my ideas in motion.

The third approach was the entrepreneurial route. This meant that I would just go for it on my own. I would create the entire concept, come up with the systems, the recipes, find the location, hire people, do everything on my own. With no experience, no money, and still with student loan debt, this would be by far the hardest and least safe route to take.

I spent the next week thinking over my three options. I mulled and mulled.

Ultimately, I decided that the philanthropic route was far too safe. I thought about both of my parents, who sacrificed their stable lives in their home countries and took the chance to move to Montreal, Canada, from India and Japan in the 1970s with no family support and just each other. Their own mother tongues were different from each other's and *still* they went for it. They took the chance *again* and moved to the United States from Montreal, when they were fifty years old so that we (their three girls) could get our green cards before turning twenty-one years old (just in case we wanted to stay in the States). For my parents to start over at fifty in a new country *again* was bold! And the sacrifice was beautiful. I made up my mind. My samurai blood was telling me not to go this safe route. I knew I would eventually be philanthropic but in different ways.

When I thought about the intrapreneurial approach, blood immediately began to rush to my head. I could hear a middle manager immediately saying something like, "No, that's not going to work," just so they don't have to deal with something else to do that might put more work on their desk or require more of their precious time. It brought back memories from my banking days. The thought of working for a company again was simply not something I was prepared to do.

So that left me with entrepreneurship. I was going to go for it. Lone-wolf style.

Holy shnikies.

My heart began to race (in a good way). It was the same feeling I had right before our soccer team walked in single file onto Cornell's Berman Field with the *Top Gun* theme song blaring on the loudspeakers right before every league game.

Battle was about to begin.

Do Cool Shit Takeaway

There are three ways to help you find an opportunity to engage your skills and passion: I call it PIE (philanthropic, intrapreneurial, entrepreneurial).

The Philanthropic Approach

Decide what you're good at, passionate about, and then think about the nonprofits/organizations that don't have access to those skill sets, marketing, branding, law, finance, etc. and where your skill sets can help those underserved communities. In the meantime, it's MB, because you're honing those skills in an environment that needs them. If you're a bit more of a cautious, risk-averse person, the philanthropic approach would be a good way to transition to entrepreneurship.

The P and I approaches are a way to get to the E, but maybe you realize that you want to stay working within an organization based on your level of comfort. If you have no experience, the philanthropic route is a great place to start because you're able to hone those skills, build your résumé, and help others. There is no right or wrong answer here! It's all about what *you* want!

The Intrapreneurial Approach

Intrapreneurship involves an effort from both the employee and the company they work for. The company should be open to allowing its employees to create from within. If you are going for this approach, you should research the company to make sure the corporate environment is conducive to your creative wants.

This means that you could basically be an entrepreneur within an existing organization. You could come up with ideas and help the company put your ideas in motion. Think about what companies are operating in an industry that you are passionate about (e.g., music, sports, publishing). Start looking for jobs in that space. Start offering your services to people who you could help. Unleash your creativity by coming up with innovative ideas that help the organization without the risk of jumping into a new business on your own.

The Entrepreneurial Approach

This is the riskiest route to take, but there is a beautiful relationship between risk and reward, right?

Think about the following before making the plunge into entrepreneurship:

- What sucks in my life that I want to change—or what doesn't exist that should?
- What products or services can I improve or change?
- Can I be passionate about this product or service for a very long time? (Because that's how long it usually takes for a venture to succeed: a very long time! The saying "It takes ten years to be an overnight success" exists for a reason.)

There is no right or wrong answer here. Everyone pushes their boundaries to different levels. Pick one approach that matches your personality best and go forward from there.

7

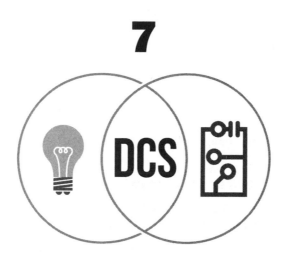

I GOT THIS

How Do I Go from Idea to Business Concept?

A few people of integrity can go a long way.
—BILL KAUTH

Why wasn't *I* invited?"

She sounded like my sister when we were in high school, whining that she wanted to join me when I went out with friends. Jenn never usually acted this way, but I could really hear how hurt she was that she was left out. I hated leaving my good friends out of interesting experiences, but this was an exception.

"Jenn! Don't feel bad at all, it's a small event. You'll find it boring anyway." I downplayed it big-time. It was actually going to be quite *awesome*. But I had to make the tough call—I had room for only eighteen people.

Jenn is sharp as a tack and one of my best friends, but as much as it seemed to be, this wasn't a social event and I had to be very strategic about who to invite.

. . . .

When I made the decision to plunge headfirst into entrepreneurship, a term my parents still didn't like (they liked the words *safe* and *doctor* a lot more), I scribbled down a few things in my notebook that I thought would be the natural steps to starting my first business and arrived at a short list of four:

Step 1: Research everything I can about the pizza business and natural-food sector.
Step 2: Talk to all of the smartest people I know in different industries about my business idea and get their input.
Step 3: Shadow someone who is successfully doing what I want to be doing (or something similar) to make sure I know what I'm getting myself into.
Step 4: Conduct an unbiased survey to see if there is truly a demand for the service I plan to provide.

STEP 1: Research everything I can about the pizza business and natural-food sector.

To begin, I thought about all my skills that I could apply to this new business idea. I knew I could manage a project from start to finish and work within tight deadlines, since I had previously worked in the film business with similar "I need it yesterday" kind of deadlines. This experience would certainly be useful.

I could do the accounting stuff, since I learned the basics in my banking days, but I also knew that it should be easy enough to figure out that sales had to outweigh expenses in order for a business to work. I mean, right?

I knew how to create and work with a cohesive team, since I had played high-level soccer for so long and had studied the way my coach picked the players who worked best together for the team.

And I knew for certain that I could remain passionate about this idea because I. Loved. Food. My first word wasn't *mama* or *dada*, it was *cookie*. (True story. I'm super health-conscious, but I've always had such a soft spot for sweets.)

It seemed perfectly natural that I should choose to start a business that focused on entertaining people. I loved hosting, and food was always at the center of my childhood. I always loved it when I was younger and my parents' friends came over to our house, ate culturally diverse foods, and shared stories.

My sisters and I grew up attending Indian and Japanese functions constantly, and we hosted a lot of these events at our house, which was always amusing for us. It was funny because the Japanese community and Indian communities are so different and yet our family fit right into both. My Japanese mom wore an Indian *salvar* (traditional Indian wear for women) when she went to Indian functions and got into the culture by learning the customs and even some recipes (she made killer chickpea curry, so Indian ladies gave her props). At Japanese functions, my Indian dad was the guy making the rice balls with seaweed (called *onigiri*). It just worked wonderfully for our family and nobody batted an eye.

Being a naturally unconventional thinker, I was especially passionate about the idea of disrupting an entire sector in the food industry and challenging the norm of conventional pizza making by creating a healthy (and delicious) alternative.

When I finished Step 1 and graduated from "Google University" (a.k.a. logging countless hours searching and researching my idea on Google), I was confident that I had a viable business idea. The healthy-living sector was beating out all major stock indexes and Whole Foods and other natural-food stores were booming. Yet the pizza industry was still stuffing their crusts with more cheese and pepperoni, still clearly in the dark about what was happening in the natural-food sector. This was exciting!

STEP 2: Talk to all of the smartest people I know in different industries about my business idea and get their input.

Next, I e-mailed and called friends and acquaintances who I thought were smart and who had started successful businesses of their own. I told them that I wanted to pick their brains about an idea that I had. A few were amenable to meet up for coffee during their lunch breaks and some were cool giving me a few minutes on the phone.

I was learning a little bit from the conversations that I had, but I wasn't moving the needle as fast as I needed to in order to set up the business. There was so much more research to be done, and I still didn't know anything about the restaurant business. When you're starting a business where you see a gap in the marketplace or a need that can be filled, you have to move quickly so no one else beats you to the punch. As much as possible, you want to be first to market.

This proved to be one of the most challenging steps in the process.

I wrote down my questions:

- What would my restaurant look and feel like?
- How could I set my pizza place apart from all the others in New York City?
- What should it be called?
- What should the menu consist of?
- How much money do I need to get the business off the ground?
- What do I want my brand to look like?
- What is the best neighborhood in which to open it?

Then I made a list of the types of people who could help me to answer these questions: architect, designer, creative director for an advertising agency, brand manager, chef, financial analyst, entrepreneur, real estate agent, and finally, a native New Yorker who knew the soul of the city.

Wow, that was a lot of questions and a lot of experts I needed to contact. It would have taken me much more time than I had to set up meetings with every one of these people. And who knows if they'd even *want* to get together? I hadn't gotten a great response rate in my first few attempts.

What if I could create a "Meeting of the Minds" where I could get all of these types of people in one room to discuss the various aspects of my business plan?

I thought about the team powwows we used to have for soccer, where we would all get in a room together to come up with a game plan to beat the other team, knowing who the strong and weak players were on that week's opposing team, and how we could use that knowledge to develop a winning strategy. We would get more and more excited as the strategy became clear and the various strengths of each person were highlighted. There was a burst of energy in this collective awareness and, man, by game day we'd be ready to kick some butt! The tricky thing in this case was to get a group of people (some of whom I wasn't particularly close with) to get super excited about someone else's business plan.

Another factor to consider when crafting my list of invitees was to get a certain *type* of person in the room for this brainstorming session. This person had to be generous with their ideas, generally successful in their career and life, and just willing to help and offer fresh ideas to someone who was creating a business.

Now, how to make this prospect appealing to my brainstorming team? I thought about what would make me want to spend my time sitting in a room talking about someone else's business idea for free. Ah! The Indian and Japanese functions from my childhood days popped in my mind. The biggest draws for me to these parties was, of course, the *free food* but also the opportunity to make new friends and explore a new aesthetic environment.

So the best way to get smart, creative, and generous people in a room together, to spend a whole night thinking and talking about my business, was to create a really fun, engaging experience where smart, interesting people could get to know one another; eat free, delicious food; and let the energy in the room build into great ideas for my business! Everyone would win. It would be an MB experience.

I spent a solid week e-mailing the various people in the different industries I hoped would attend. I explained to them that it was going to be a very *private* and *exclusive* Meeting of the Minds. I told them to expect a special invitation via e-mail in one week's time. I hoped the mysteriousness of the e-mail and the fact that they would have to wait a week to receive it would help raise the excitement.

Once I started getting some positive e-mail responses back, and knew that there would be at least more than one person attending, I had to find a great venue to host the gathering.

I began calling every single person I knew who I thought had access to *any* venue (a cool apartment, private room, loft space, or a unique office—anywhere that had a bit of character). The most important thing was that it had to be free to use the space. There was no way I could afford renting a venue, so I had to find someone who'd be OK lending me a cool spot for free. I employed the old MB rule, and when calling around to ask friends, I made sure to let them know that if they could secure the location for me, they would be invited to the event and would have the opportunity to meet and network with a great group of people. Not to mention, they'd score a free dinner!

After a couple of days of searching, one of my friends called me back and said that he'd let me use the boardroom at MTV Studios. Thank goodness! I was starting to wonder if I'd have to organize a picnic in Central Park instead. (And while it would have been a free and cool alternative spot, I'd be at the mercy of the weather.)

I put together a personal e-card, the front of which said:

> *You have been handpicked as one of eighteen people to attend the private "Meeting of the Minds" gathering that will be held at the exclusive MTV Studios. Dinner, drinks, and creative conversation will be included.*

Inside the card, I wrote:

> *Tonight's discussion topic is one that will engage every one of your senses and may disrupt an entire industry after this night is over.*

I am talking about transforming the classic pizza place into a healthy, local, and sustainable eatery, and I am looking to answer some questions that will help give birth to this new idea. You are critical in making this possible.

Please come to this meeting with answers to these questions:

- *What is the most memorable restaurant experience you've ever had and why?*

- *If you were to come up with a new way to present a well-known product like pizza, what would it look like?*

We all share great memories eating a slice of pizza, and I want you to enter this meeting remembering the feelings associated with sharing a pizza pie with your friends and loved ones.

I look forward to receiving your RSVPs by tomorrow end of day. We are looking at Wednesday, June 15, at 7:00 p.m. or Thursday, June 16, at 7:00 p.m. Please include your preferred date.

In (healthy) pizza we trust,
Miki

I hit SEND. I repeated this twenty more times by sending personal e-mails to my twenty "top tier" people I wanted to come. I figured that I'd send it to the people I really wanted to come first and then fill in the gaps later.

I sat in front of the computer, reread my message a hundred times (you know you do it too after you create an important message!), and waited. Nothing happened in the first hour. I refreshed my in-box so many times, it was a bit silly (and, yes, slightly obsessive compulsive). I wanted to make sure that the server wasn't holding messages hostage! Still nothing. So I ordered cheeseless pizza. Obviously.

After the second hour, my mail beeped. I finally had my first message from one of the people I really wanted to come.

"I'd be delighted to! Thank you for thinking of me! I pick Wednesday over Thursday."

Yes!!!! One down! Then all of a sudden, messages started flooding into my in-box.

"Sounds like fun. I pick Wednesday."

"I love pizza. Count me in. I prefer Thursday over Wednesday."

And it went on. By midday the following day, sixteen out of the twenty said yes! I was thrilled.

Do Cool Shit Takeaway

Always remember to put yourself in the other person's shoes and figure out what would make *you* say yes to something before you approach someone else. Frame the conversation in such a way to see benefit for *them* for attending something for *you*.

For example do not say: "I am excited to invite you to a Meeting of the Minds event with eighteen of the most interesting people in New York City . . . blah blah."

"I'm excited" still means "me" being excited . . . it must be about *them*. Remember, the invite said:

"*You* have been handpicked as one of eighteen people [make it about them] to attend the private Meeting of the Minds gathering [private is always good] that will be held at the exclusive MTV Studios [exclusive is also good]. Dinner, drinks, and creative conversation will be included [free food is so important]."

If you make it about them and not you, you will have much more success at getting the attendance you want.

After countless hours of planning and preparing, the day finally came. I didn't expect everyone to show up, but I smiled with gratitude as one by one, my guests strolled in.

I brought in healthy salads, some seasonal appetizers, flatbreads from a high-end pizzeria down the street (for inspiration), and blood orange sorbet with fresh berries and whipped cream for dessert, and I'd placed a big white writing pad up on an easel so that once the ideas started flowing, I could get them down quickly and have something to refer to later.

As everyone milled around before sitting down, they began to introduce themselves to one another. It was great watching them laugh and then pull out their cell phones to exchange their contact info. This was starting out great.

But then, I had a crisis of confidence. I got inside my head and felt myself start to stumble. I had been so excited to get to this moment of gathering industry experts in one room and now that everyone was here, I felt queasy. What if I had trouble leading a productive session? This was my one shot to get important input from these people. Or worse, what if the brainstorming consensus was that my idea sucked?

I took a few minutes for myself to look at my notes, gather my thoughts, and take a few deep breaths to calm down. My cheeks flushed and my heart raced. It was time to start the meeting.

I asked everyone to please take a seat. I thanked them for coming and briefly introduced the concept. My voice shook a bit. Thankfully, I had my cheat sheet, which consisted of my list of questions to ask and my talking points. "This is really important," I thought. "Just keep going."

So I did.

First I had everyone go around the room, introduce themselves, and say one line about why they love pizza. That really helped break the ice for everyone, but especially for me, since talking about my love for pizza and food in general was so easy to do!

Once we got in our groove, we went around the room and talked about the questions I had everyone answer from the invitation, and as we went, people threw out ideas. Creative juices naturally began to flow, with eighteen sharp and unique minds connecting and adding additional viewpoints on top of one another's thoughts. We could have broken the group up into even smaller groups (like we used to do in college), but I liked the fact that everyone in the room could hear what everyone else was saying and could spark more thoughts and ideas faster.

Over the course of five hours (everyone got so into it that they stayed for five hours!), the energy in the room built and built. It was beautiful to watch.

We hashed out a lot of the main ideas:

The name

SLICE: The perfect food—The best idea to name the restaurant *SLICE* was chosen because we wanted to make our place reminiscent of the classic New York pizza slice. The tagline "the perfect food" highlighted for our consumers what was different about our place. The thought behind the tagline was that if prepared with local and healthful ingredients, a slice of pizza is, in fact, *the perfect food*. It's tasty and healthy, the perfect balance of carbs, veggies, and protein. (Again, I should remind you that we have since changed the name to *WILD*, after seven years of enjoying the name *SLICE*. We are expanding to Vegas and beyond, and since there were pizza places called "Slice" all over the country, we wanted something more distinctive. Not to mention, we couldn't outright own the name Slice. Now we're truly branded.)

The logo concept and the unique way of cutting our slices

In the brainstorm, the best idea came from a simple drawing of a triangle divided into four smaller triangles. The thought here was that we wanted to maintain the integrity of the shape of the classic slice of pizza but, again, offer a unique twist to it. The new and improved way of presenting a slice would be the "diamond cut" of four smaller triangular slices so that it could (a) promote sharing of different flavors among friends and (b) slow down the process of inhaling a slice of pizza, which is what usually happens. By cutting up the pizza into four bite-size pieces, it would allow the brain to catch up to a full stomach and thus not overeat. Also, this triangle design would be a unique logo mark that would be memorable and catchy. (Again, the logo has also since been updated to fit the elevated *WILD* brand.)

The way we were going to design our pizza boxes

One of the ideas that came from this was that the standard pizza box was big, cumbersome, and frustrating to deal with once the pie was done. Also, if there were leftovers, it would be frustrating to try and store the pizza box in the fridge, let alone inside of a recycling garbage can. So we made the box a longer rectangular shape, slimmer to the eye (denoting a "healthier" experience versus a "fatter" pizza box), easy to store in the fridge, and easy to drop in the recycling bin.

The interior design look and feel

The best idea was to go with the brand identity of sustainable and all-natural, reclaimed materials, bamboo wall and flooring (as bamboo is an eco-friendly sustainable material), and to use existing structural walls (like brick walls) to our advantage as design elements.

When you have a roomful of different experts from different industries, everyone has a different way of approaching this business, so all of the different approaches were investigated and fresh ideas came from them. I felt like everyone in the room learned about how other people in other industries deconstructed the same concept and picked up different parts.

Once this meeting was over, I felt like my idea finally had legs. It felt like a real business for the first time.

Do Cool Shit Takeaway

At the brainstorming session, you must have as many questions on your list answered and get as detailed as you can within each section while you have the group of experts in the room together. The more you can keep people on track to answer your questions in as much detail as possible, the more you will get out of it. You may have to be kind of a (polite) hard-ass to keep everyone focused, but this is your one shot to pump the experts for knowledge, and you have to make the most of it.

STEP 3: Shadow someone who is successfully doing what I want to be doing (or something similar) to make sure I know what I'm getting myself into.

Sometimes, you'll have to rely on distant or tenuous connections in order to get things done. Case in point: my sister's boyfriend's sister was really good friends with the wife of one of the most successful restaurateurs in New York City: Rich Wolf. (Did you follow that? Yeah, me neither.) He owned the hugely popular restaurant Tao in Midtown. If there was one person I wanted to follow, it was *him*. He ran the restaurant scene in New York and was known to be one of the best.

One evening when I knew Rich was going to be at his restaurant (sister's boyfriend's sister told me), I decided to go and pay him a visit and see if I could convince him to let me follow him around for a month or so and observe and help him operate his business.

As I got to Tao, and walked past the iconic giant Buddha statue in the middle of the dining room, I said a little prayer to him to give me the strength to approach Rich with confidence.

I scanned the room and spotted the booth where Rich was sitting. I had googled him earlier in the evening, so I knew what he looked like. He was with his wife and four guests. He didn't know who I was, and I hadn't called ahead to schedule this meeting. I was going to have to create the opportunity myself. I watched them for a while and waited for the most opportune moment to go over. I knew that there was generally a lull immediately after the waiter takes a table's order. That was my moment.

I took a deep breath and walked up to their table. I introduced myself first to Rich's wife, since she was the person with whom I had my Six Degrees of Kevin Bacon–style connection. I said, "Hi! I know your friend Lisa! She told me how amazing you are and I just really wanted to meet you!" She was gracious and seemed excited to meet me as well. Basically, she couldn't deny me even if she wanted to. I let peer pressure work in my favor.

After a few words were exchanged, she introduced me to her husband. I told him how much I loved Tao and how proud I was of him. (I often find myself saying things like "I'm proud of you." It implies familial bond, like a proud parent or proud child.)

I told him that I had heard about the new small-plates restaurant that he was opening called Stanton Social in the Lower East Side and that I knew he was probably incredibly busy dealing with all of his current restaurants *and* with opening the new place. I briefly explained to him about my own business plan and asked if I could help him out for a little while for free and in return, I'd get to see what the day-to-day was like in the restaurant business. It would be win-win and definitely MB.

I think he probably felt a bit on-the-spot with his wife and friends right there watching, but regardless, he agreed! Yes! I was so excited! I got his phone number and business card, thanked his wife again, and walked out of there as fast as I could, before he could change his mind.

Knowing the importance of acting fast and seizing the opportunity when it arises, the very next day I called him and he said I should meet him the following day at his new restaurant location. The next day, he still remembered me (thank G), so I spent the next month following him around when he had meetings he thought were valuable for me to see (team management meetings, architect meetings, chef tastings, design meetings, construction meetings). He was very generous with his time and was patient with me. I will forever be grateful to him.

One thing that became immediately apparent after shadowing Rich was that I wasn't ready to open a big place. His places seemed so intimidating; it took an army to run them. I wanted (and frankly needed) to start small. I decided that my place would at least start off as a counter-service pizza restaurant and not have a waitstaff. I didn't want to overreach in the early stages.

Do Cool Shit Takeaway

Do whatever it takes to find the person you aspire to be like (in business) and shadow them if you can. Read up about them and find out where they like to eat or like to go out and then "accidentally run into them" (*stalking* is also a good term to use here) and then go for it (don't wait for your nerves to catch up to you). This is such an important step in figuring out if you really are cut out to start your own version of this business or not, so there is no time to be shy here. Be bold!

While you're shadowing the person, really take notice of everything they do and be honest with yourself about what you think you can manage for workload. You may need to start very simply and ramp up. This is part of the reason you are following the other successful expert in the first place—to see at what level *you* are capable of succeeding at your starting point. You can certainly dream big and think big, but if you start big, you may fail big. Starting small can help you get going and you can ramp up from there as you gain confidence in your abilities. Then go as big as you want!

STEP 4: Conduct an unbiased survey to see if there is truly a demand for the service I plan to provide.

That didn't take long. As I went around with Rich, and everywhere I went, I would survey the people around me. I asked them these questions:

- Do you like pizza?
- Do you eat more or less pizza than you did in the past?
- Would you eat more pizza if it was made with healthy, organic ingredients?

Overall, the resounding feedback was *yes*! Almost everyone would eat more pizza if it was made with better, healthier ingredients. The gluten-free and vegan communities were especially excited that I'd be offering alternatives as well.

Once I had these experiences and conducted the necessary experiments, I felt like I was equipped with what I needed to take my new business to the next level. Even Rich thought it was a good idea, which gave me hope.

I had done my due diligence. Now it was go time. Now I needed to raise money for my new business venture.

8

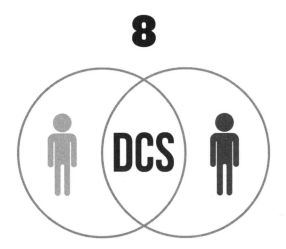

BUSINESS PLANS DON'T RAISE DOLLARS, *PEOPLE* DO

Why Connecting Is the Key to Money

*Recognize that the harder you work and the better prepared
you are, the more luck you might have.*

—ED BRADLEY

My palms were sweaty. I had worked so hard to get to this moment. I focused on looking professional and not having a nervous expression on my face, but it was hard to cover up my anticipation.

Was he really going to write the check for $25,000 to help fund my new business? Or was I going to have to go back to square one and try to find funding elsewhere?

Let me back up a second and tell you how I got here.

I was twenty-five years old and had never raised money before. When

I worked in investment banking and then after that, in television, I was paid the same salary every two weeks and never had to even think about that side of the business.

Now that I finally had to think about it, it was so weird and wonderful to see people buying into fresh, entrepreneurial ideas, and to experience raising money firsthand made me a true believer in the American risk-taking mentality.

I have to admit that it took me quite some time to figure out how to significantly increase the likelihood of getting people to say, "Yes, I believe in this, and I believe in you. I want to invest, please."

Believe you me, my first several attempts were nothing short of humiliating.

I would put on a suit (dusted one off from my banking days—I wondered if they could tell), and would meet the various potential investors at any one of the ubiquitous Starbucks around the city (being in a public setting was less intimidating than a pin-drop quiet conference room—although I tried that too). When I would meet them, I would smile and laugh, trying to soften the intensity of the situation for me, and I always offered to buy them coffee. (Maybe a little kick of caffeine would get them to pull out their checkbooks faster? Nope that didn't work either.)

When I sat down with them, I didn't have a lot of the answers to the questions they asked because it was my first time pitching my own business and I wasn't exactly sure what would be addressed in the meeting. I realized I sounded nervous and by sounding nervous, it made me even more nervous. Looking back, I should have written down every single possible question and rebuttal from an investor's standpoint and had the answers ready before going to the meetings.

In my opinion, raising money is one of those things that nobody truly enjoys doing (unless you're raising money for someone else or for a cause). It's hard to find investors, it screws with your ego, screws with confidence, usually takes so much more time than you imagined, and it's total agony to wait while potential investors make up their minds. It's one of the most challenging issues for any passion project. We have to remember that investors are people too and they have the right to be indecisive, and all we can do is put our best, most confident foot forward and reassure them that their investment is safe.

Raising money can also be one of the most exciting experiences. When someone hands you a check because they believe in you and they believe in what you are pouring your heart into, it validates everything!

The traditional way to raise money is to put a lengthy business plan together and do a formal pitch to potential investors (i.e., anyone who may have a little extra cash sitting in the bank collecting dust *and* is willing to listen). You have probably figured this out already, but I'm not a traditional person. I never put a lengthy business plan together. Instead, I created a slideshow presentation made up of mostly images, which I could then augment with my presentation. (As I've said before, a picture is worth a thousand words.)

Now I'm not saying that putting together a seventy-five-page business plan isn't necessary eventually and shows diligence, it's just that, in the moment, it's not only about that. (Except when you are working for an investment bank or trying to raise $200 million like my friend Michael, then you may need that seventy-five-page business plan. Raising fewer than $500,000 in $5,000 to $10,000 increments requires a different strategy in my opinion.)

One of the main reasons that people invest is not just that they think the idea is really strong but that they have a strong belief in the person(s) who is going to execute the idea. You must show total confidence in your idea. "Fake it till you make it" is an important tactic, especially at the beginning.

After trying many different ways to get people to buy into my idea, like one-on-one dinners, lunch meetings, formal meetings in office conference rooms (the list goes on), I realized that I needed a much more comfortable approach that worked for *me*.

At this point, I had months of failed attempts under my belt. I took about a week to reflect on why it wasn't working out and then I realized that I was so uncomfortable in one-on-one situations. I just wasn't my usual high-energy bubbly self.

I then thought about the situations I was most comfortable in, where I showed my most natural, engaging self. I was most comfortable with my friends and family and also thrived in group settings. I was best at parties and events and I was definitely most natural at bringing people together.

I kept coming back to all of our family dinners with the Japanese and Indian communities and how my sister and I would get everyone excited to attend. I remembered how fun our birthday parties were because they were unique—we always added at least one fun twist (there would be current-events quizzes, talent shows, races, and songs), and it made people really want to be invited back the following year.

I had created a successful brainstorming event for the restaurant just a few months prior and it had had a resoundingly positive response rate. Why didn't I even think to apply that idea to raising money? If it ain't broke, don't fix it! I couldn't believe I'd wasted six months of awful meetings when I could have created a single event with the purpose of raising money.

If I could put together a few great dinner parties, give people a taste of my new good-for-you pizzas, and present my idea in a fun environment where wine flowed in a great setting, I would win over the entire crowd and get more than one investor on board in a single night, instead of doing time-consuming one-on-one meetings.

So I followed these basic steps to start the process of collecting investment dollars.

CREATE AN EXCITING EVENT

Getting a group to think an idea is good is a lot more powerful and potent than getting one person to agree to the idea. The energy around the idea is what's palpable and interesting to people. When you are looking around a room and seeing people nodding and engaged, it's much easier to pull out your checkbook than if nobody is around, right?

So the execution of this event is critical. If it's not executed properly, then it will have the exact opposite effect: everyone together will decide not to do it.

To ensure that your execution is flawless, here is what I did to make the event a success:

Bring a chef who can prepare food that will excite the senses and leave people satisfied.

If you don't have a lot of money and, er, maybe don't even know how to cook, ask a friend who loves to cook and has cooked for larger parties before to prepare a dinner-party meal. Tell them that you will provide all the ingredients and tools and that you will take great photos of the food.

For five minutes of the evening, let your chef friend have the floor to talk about a project that he or she is interested in or working on. This will give them another personal reason to cook for this important event. Again, this goes back to the MB philosophy of mutually beneficial experiences.

If all of your friends are challenged in the cooking department, you can now go to a place like kitchit.com, where you can hire personal chefs for a very reasonable price who will shop/prepare/serve the food for your dinner party. I definitely recommend this option if you can spare a bit of cash.

If you want to cook the meal yourself, that is fine, but then have a friend or hire someone to come and serve the entire meal. You do *not* want to be running around getting people food when you are trying to get in your zone and be the founder of your new business. This ties back into the idea that you have to have confidence and appear in control. Rather, you are an expert in this chosen field (in my case, the restaurant business). Not to mention, it looks pretty awesome when you have someone waiting on all of your guests while you host the dinner.

Should you or a friend decide to prepare the meal, here is a great sample menu. Expect to spend between $300 and $400 for a party of fifteen people.

BEVERAGES

- 1 white wine option (chardonnay)
- 1 red wine option (cabernet franc)
- 1 vodka cocktail (perhaps a ginger lemonade with vodka—this way people can also have it virgin if they don't want to drink. Plus, who doesn't love a great homemade ginger lemonade?)
- coffee/tea with milks/sugars

APPETIZER

- Fresh arugula salad with goat cheese, cherry tomatoes, and roasted sunflower seeds, with a light balsamic vinaigrette
- Hummus, kalamata olives, and olive oil, with fresh cucumbers and warm pitas

ENTRÉE (FOR ME, IT WAS HEALTHY PIZZAS; FOR YOU, IT COULD BE SOMETHING LIKE THIS.)

- Vegetarian curry entrée (You can pick up great curry sauce at any market.)
- Free-range chicken and vegetables over brown rice mixed together in a coconut sauce.
- When things are mixed together like curries and chicken and rice dishes, you don't have to worry about the food losing its heat when plating, and it makes it more "family style"

DESSERT

- A scoop of fruit sorbet and chocolate chip cookies
- Fresh fruit with honey and fresh whipped cream (You can easily make homemade whipped cream in ten minutes.)

Get a cool venue to host the event.
To save money, call any of your friends who live or work in a cool, memorable place and explain that you want to cohost a dinner party with them and that you will bring really interesting people together who they will want to meet.

When I say "cool, memorable place," I mean one of the following:

- a well-designed industrial loft apartment
- a spacious house with a big family-style table that you can deck out with candles and flowers
- an apartment with a patio so dinner can be served outdoors
- an exposed-brick apartment where you can put candles along the walls to create a really nice ambiance
- a party room in a friend's apartment building
- a rooftop space
- a country-club library room

Get press to attend (TV, print, Web).
Getting any kind of press to attend your event will have two benefits: it will publicize your business and get people buzzing about it, and it will impress the potential investors.

I managed to get the Food Network to not only attend the dinner party but to also follow me for four months with the intention of producing a TV show focused on my business.

I sent an e-mail out to everyone I knew who may know someone who works in television. Even if you just know an assistant, they can sometimes pass your e-mail along to a more senior producer or editor.

I sent a Food Network producer a mysterious e-mail saying that I had an idea for the network's show *Recipe for Success* and that it would be a huge win-win (an MB experience) for both of us.

The producer called me back! Somehow, when she got me on the phone I was able to talk through my nervousness and tell her that she had an opportunity to create a highly rated television show on the Food Network. This show would follow a young first-time entrepreneur and it would be great television because I didn't know what I was doing and that I would screw up a *lot*! After all, I was in the process of opening up a healthy pizza restaurant in New York City, a city where there are so many other pizza places and 95 percent of restaurants close in their first year and 85 percent of restaurants close in their second year. I told them that I was a first-time businessperson, it was my first time working in a restaurant, and that this show will be the train-wreck show they've been waiting for. Reality TV is all about chaos, and I would give them chaos on a silver pizza tray.

The Food Network bought the idea! The next thing I knew, they were following me around, attending my investor dinner parties, and documenting the entire process! Part of me was freaking out about it, but I played along as best as I could. They followed me around for those four months and the show *Recipe for Success: Pizza Girl* aired on repeat more than fifteen times internationally because it was such a hit! You can find the episode on my YouTube page: www.youtube.com/user/mikiagrawal.

Make a cool slideshow.

My slideshow covered the basics that an investor would want to know, and this time around, I knew what to expect and was ready for all of their questions:

- What is the problem in the marketplace?
- How big is the potential market?

- What is the idea?
- How does this idea solve the problem?
- Who is my target audience?
- Who are my competitors?
- How will I position my idea in the marketplace and gain a loyal client base?
- What are my revenue projections?
- What is the payback structure? (i.e., How will investors get paid back?)

Get someone else to present your idea for you if you get nervous giving presentations.

There is nothing worse than spending weeks and months organizing a fundraising event and then bombing the whole thing when you have to get up to present your business idea and not coming across as a confident speaker. When you sound like a not-so-confident speaker, it may make potential investors think you'll be a not-so-confident leader.

Through my research and pitching, I noticed that sometimes other people explained my business just as well as I did, if not better. I was so deep into the process and wanted to say so much about my restaurant that it was sometimes easier for someone else to clearly distill my concept in a few easy-to-understand sentences.

I also knew that I was best at connecting with people in a relaxed setting and my most natural self came out when I wasn't presenting my idea formally in front of people. My posh British friend, Richard (the one who branded the original Slice concept), agreed to give my presentation at the upcoming fundraising dinner and I would be there simply to answer questions and be the cheerleader for my idea. This accomplished two things:

- It made the business look more *professional*. It showed I'd already begun collaborating with someone and had won someone over to join my team.

- It gave me a chance to be my most authentic self. The more you can put yourself in a situation where your most authentic and natural self shines through, the better your success rate.

Do Cool Shit Takeaway

Always have an *ask* and *action* in mind for the potential investor or buyer of your product/art/mission at the event itself. You'll want to get an answer (positive, hopefully!) as soon after they've been dazzled as possible. Every day after that, it becomes a tougher sell because they'll remember less and less about their experience. If your event is unique and memorable enough, your guests will be more likely to get on board with your business idea right away.

When people's hearts and minds are open, they are the most giving. Here are some ways to get your guests to open their hearts and minds:

- Give everyone an opportunity to share a piece of him- or herself. Have a storytelling segment at your event where everyone can share a one- to two-minute story that relates to your theme of the night. At the end of the day, everyone wants to be heard. Everyone has stories to tell. Everyone wants to be recognized. Even if people are shy, if coaxed enough times to share, they will be so happy they did in the end and will go home feeling so energized and excited to tell their friends.

- Make the event/fund-raiser/dinner party interactive. It shouldn't be just a one-way conversation. You can do this by having different product pieces on the walls of the venue to get people talking and interacting. You can also place questions or clues on the wall to facilitate conversation. You goal is to get as many people walking around smiling, conversing, and having a good time.

Use the following as examples to create an *ask* or *action* item:

- Create a memorable postcard-size "pledge card." This should be positioned at every place setting during the dessert portion of the evening. By this time, you and your idea would have hopefully won over everyone. The pledge card is used to close the deal.

  For example, a pledge card for potential restaurant investors would say: "*I pledge* to support the creators of delicious, healthy, and environmentally friendly comfort food. Please write your name, e-mail addresses, pledge amount, and a haiku about your favorite comfort food." Always include something silly that makes people laugh. Make this pledge card memorable and creative. Add sparkles.

- At the end of the night, give all of your guests one to two small creative gifts that they can then give to friends they think might also pledge their support. Maybe you give them beautiful rocks that you found on the beach and painted with an inspirational word. Maybe it's a simple card that you handwrite to each person for a personal touch. This is a great way to grow your potential investor pool in a manageable way. Ultimately, people who invest in you or your idea should genuinely like you and want to spend time with you. Try and honor that as best as you can.

- If you are hosting an event or fund-raiser, try to keep them small at first so that you can build traction. This will allow everyone to share a story about something relating to food or art or business or whatever it is you are trying to grow. Investors want to be heard, they want to share stories, and they want to be recognized.

- Call everyone you know who has the ability to invest in a new business. Start with those people who have large networks, since they may be able to bring others on board.

  Knowing people who can invest in ideas is so important. If you don't know anyone like that, it's time to go to events where you think potential investors may frequent. Start early, because it can take some time to make these connections. Think about all the places in your area where the wealthier community spends time. Golf courses, horse races, and fund-raisers.

- Go to TED.com and see if there are of the local TEDx talks in your area. Find out when angel investor conferences will be and where they will be hosted. (In case you may not be familiar with the term, an *angel investor* is an individual who provides capital for a business start-up, usually in exchange for ownership equity.) If you can't get into the event, research the hotel bars or conference areas where the event is being held and make an appearance! Check out entrepreneurial events like the Startup Weekend (startupweekend.com), and see if you can apply to get into the conference for free. Go to special events at collaborative office spaces where angel investors come in and meet young start-ups. Basically, put yourself where the action is and that's where you'll find the money!

CONNECTING IS *NOT* NETWORKING

The most important thing I learned when it came to raising money was how to connect on a deeper level with people and investors in a way that made them want to be a part of a greater community rather than just a monetary investment.

If you connect with people in a sincere way, raising money becomes no longer about the massive and thorough business plan as much as a well-thought-out idea executed by someone who is smart, likable, and excited.

Networking is just plain uncomfortable. You walk around a room reading name tags and seeing if the other people walking around looking at name tags could be useful to you. You exchange fancy business cards (just like in the movie *American Psycho*, and we all know what came of *those* card exchanges!). When you're networking, it's all about "What do you do?" and "Where do you work?" I've built more comfortable and effective relationships with people via the very basic NST rule: no small talk.

Questions like "Where are you from?" and "What do you do?" don't inspire people to really connect with you. Here is how to use NST to help you to connect quickly with people:

Ask pointed, more personal questions.

For example: "What are you most excited about?" or "What's the next big thing coming up in your life?" or my favorite "What's your dream?" It's open-ended, and the conversation can go anywhere.

Most often I see that people immediately open up and show their true colors, energy, and excitement when they're talking about their dreams, what they're excited about, and what they are eager to change and work on. Once you get them talking about these things, the conversation naturally creates a shimmer of excitement to it, and it's from that excitement that a stronger relationship can begin to grow.

Listen and genuinely show a lot of interest in the person you are connecting with.

People in general have short attention spans, and at events like these, it can be tough to make an impression.

If you truly listen to someone and are present in the conversation, people will feel good and want to continue to be around you because it's apparent that you genuinely are interested in what they have to say. It's natural that people feel connected to you when you honor their inherent desire to feel heard. The only time this hasn't worked for me is when the person takes your enthusiasm to be an indication of their own greatness . . . and when that's the case, who needs *them*?

Ask follow-up questions that incorporate their answers to show that you were listening.

Reflecting back what they say not only validates them and shows that you were listening, but it also makes them feel good about opening up to you and they will start to loosen up and connect with you.

Showing genuine interest in others, listening, and showing excitement in what you are working on yourself, is the quickest way to really connect and get them to develop a relationship with you that could then become something mutually beneficial in the future.

EXCITEMENT IS MAGNETIC

When it came to my business, I was always excited about sharing my idea. I had endless energy when it came to talking and discussing my idea and it rubbed off on my friends, colleagues, and everyone I met.

It's even more fun to belong to an exciting group of people doing exciting things. There is real magnetism around excitement. Most people aren't super pumped about their jobs and to find someone so excited about their idea is refreshing.

The first time I met one of my investors, it was on his second date with his girlfriend (now wife) while they were about to sit down to dinner at a restaurant. I remember they were up at the bar, sitting on two of the stools, and there was an open stool beside them. I was also waiting for a table, so I sat down. I broke the ice by commenting on what a nice-looking couple they seemed to be. When all else fails, rely on a compliment! We started to talk and I asked them about how they met and got really excited to hear about their new relationship. I started to talk about how fun relationships are early on (they are!), and, mind you, I had no intention to raise money from him; I didn't even know he had the opportunity to invest in businesses. I was simply genuinely interested in their lives. He then asked me what I was up to and I excitedly told him about my new project. My enthusiasm was so contagious that he asked me to send him some more information about it.

The next day I sent him the slideshow presentation, and he got back to me to say he was very interested. We met up a couple more times over a few meals, lots of laughter, and the beginning of what is now an eight-year friendship. And I raised a sizable investment from him.

He actually called money "energy" and said, "I am giving you energy to grow your business." I loved this way of looking at it, and I couldn't have agreed more. This money would give me some of the energy and movement I needed to get started in my business.

I continued meeting and connecting with people, and I ended up raising the $250,000 I needed to get my business up and running.

Do Cool Shit Tip

In order to collect the checks from angel investors, you need to set up an LLC (go to your bank, they can set it up for you) and create a simple term sheet with an operating agreement for the investors to sign. (You can find a sample term sheet and standard operating agreement on docoolshit.org.)

At this point, I had just turned twenty-six years old and was ready to get the doors open to my new venture and let the next chapter of my adventure unfold. Raising money had been my biggest challenge thus far, but I knew it was just the beginning. The odds were stacked high against me, but I was ready to prove them wrong.

Do Cool Shit Tip

An exciting new alternative to recruiting angel investors is crowd funding. *Wikipedia* describes crowd funding as "the collective effort of individuals who network and pool their money, usually via the Internet, to support efforts initiated by other people or organizations." Using platforms like kickstarter.com, indiegogo.com, catapult.org, you do not need to give any equity away. You will simply receive "preorders" or donations. You can also apply for seed funding at places like goldenseeds.com and startups.co.

9

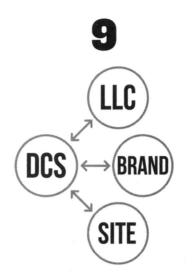

GET SHIT DONE FAST

How to Get Your Business Open Without Wasting Time

Creativity starts with a little touch of insanity and culminates with the highest trust on its beauty, but throughout it maintains the hands of originality and humanity.

—Anuj Somany

Sixty-five thousand dollars!? It would cost that much to create the branding package for my new business? Are you kidding me!?

That was more than a quarter of my entire budget, and I hadn't even built anything yet, let alone put a down payment on a location. We were like newborns just out of the womb with the umbilical cord still attached. We hadn't even taken our first breath. That $65,000 proposal from the branding company was simply not an option, but I desperately needed a clear branding vision. What was I going to do?

. . . .

It had taken me about seven months to finally raise $250,000 from angel investors (i.e., friends, friends of friends, former colleagues, and random angels I met in New York over a couple of years). I now had the general concept of my business mapped out from the brainstorming sessions I held and I was ready for the next step.

With the help of my architect we calculated that I would need at the barest of bare bones $180,000 to build out a small location—and this fee included calling on every favor I could. It wasn't exactly clear what I would be spending on a space because I didn't have a location picked out, but I was assuming I'd have a space that was smaller than five hundred square feet, and according to my architect, $180,000 was about how much it might cost. (When I look back at it now, I see that was a dangerous approach, because it's always best to estimate costs *after* you find a space.)

Rich Wolf told me that I would need to put down three months' rent on a space, plus first month's rent in advance (standard practice for commercial spaces in NYC apparently). I knew my budget wouldn't support a dollar more than $6,000 per month. Anything cheaper than that wouldn't be in a good location, according to my real estate broker friend, so it meant that I would need to put down $24,000 just to get the keys to a space. Man, New York ain't cheap!

That left me with $46,000 to do things like get my business fully branded, purchase initial food inventory, and have funds for initial staff training over a couple of weeks. This also had to include having some working capital left over—which was the important financial breathing room I needed to let the business grow into itself and gain traction without worrying about money and paying bills with revenues right off the bat. Businesses need time to ramp up.

My dad had always drilled into my head that most businesses failed if they didn't have enough runway to properly take off. (Pops has always been a fan of a good aeronautical pun.)

To clarify what I needed, I wrote down the steps I had to take before even beginning the search for the $6,000-per-month storefront in Manhattan:

- Create overall brand design.
- Design a website.
- Finalize the menu design.
- Set up social media.

First order of business: get my business branded. Once I was branded, I would have the finalized name, logo, mission statement, color schemes, fonts, restaurant look and feel, talking points, public identity, and the general aesthetic of the restaurant created in one nice, neat package. I had figured out some of this at the brainstorming sessions but not the fully detailed brand concept.

I started calling several branding agencies and met with a few of them. I explained to them that it was my first small business, I wanted to get it right, and I had budgeted $5,000 to brand my business, which seemed like a generous amount of money.

I practically spit my soy chai tea all over my computer screen when the proposals started coming back: $65,000 from one branding firm and $15,000 from another—they ran the gamut, but they were nowhere in the range I could afford. Seriously? Just to pick some fonts and colors? Good grief! (At the time, I had no idea how important this step was for a small business that had big dreams to grow, and how much creativity and time goes into making a successful brand, but still, I didn't have that kind of money.)

I decided to try a different route.

I called my good friend Richard, who was a branding expert, and told him that I would pay him in equity if he could help brand my business for free. He was the same friend who helped put my investor presentation together and had given my presentation at one of my fundraising dinner parties. He attended my main brainstorming session and finalized the name of my business and my logo. We had met many times to talk about my business and so he was already very familiar with what I was trying to do.

At this point, he was working at a branding firm and I knew he had been thinking of breaking off on his own. This could be a good trial run for him to see if he could brand something by himself as a freelancer. (Notice the old MB scenario.) He graciously accepted.

My friend Ian, an architect, had been working for a firm and was also at a place where he wanted to branch off and start something on his own, so he agreed to design my place for free in exchange for a piece of the pizza pie, so to speak.

My best friend from college, Zach (who ended up also investing in my business), had a childhood friend who was a talented interior designer. Coincidentally, she was also working for an interior design company and was ready to start branching out to start her own firm. It would be a great opportunity to add a real business to her personal portfolio, and when I offered to give her a percentage of my business in exchange, she agreed as well.

Richard and his team designed a brilliant first menu for us (go to docoolshit.org to see it). It was a twenty-page booklet that had our menu on the first and last page and the rest of it was a bunch of funny and silly images with text. It helped garner a lot of attention during our launch. He also helped us create our first website.

Other friends helped out in various ways whenever they could, and some simply did it for the fun of it and to be part of something new and exciting. It was MB all around!

Do Cool Shit Takeaway

If you're ever starting a new business, it is important to itemize all the tasks and elements that you'll need to create, and to run the list by someone who has started a similar business previously, to make sure you have all your items on the list and that

they're in the correct order. Once you've identified everything you need to create, think about your network of friends and colleagues and see who does work in that sector or field. Oftentimes, people are looking for freelance work or they are looking for opportunities to "go out on their own." Collaborating in this way is an effective and inspiring method to get important parts of your business completed, for cheap . . . and possibly even build a strategic partnership in the process.

To help keep track of all of the moving pieces and stay connected with the overall strategy, a great free online task manager is available to make your life much easier. It's called Asana (asana.com).

In the end, we came up with lots of creative ideas together. Was it perfect? Not entirely. But it stood out, it was free, and it got me started! I knew I'd pull it all together down the road (when I had real money to spend on branding). If you don't have friends who can help you get started, places like Crowdspring.com or 99designs.com are great for inexpensive branding. The biggest difference between these sites and hiring someone to brand your business is that these sites are generally a much cheaper option. You also get a lot more branding directions and options than if you were to go with a person, who will probably give you a maximum of three directions.

A FEW THOUGHTS ON BRANDING

Branding is tough! One of my very smart friends, Sam (the Intrigue Expert) (check out intrigueagency.com to see Sam's work), and her son, Andrew (visit gatsbysmile.com for examples of Andrew's work), break down branding into two parts—words and visuals:

Words

This is the language you use to tell and sell people on your business. It includes:

- Mission statement
- Pitch
- Copy within the marketing materials and press kit

Visuals

This is the part of your business that people can see and feel, and it provides the housing for your words. Visuals include:

- Website
- Social media pages
- Marketing materials
- Packaging
- Physical store

If you know how to talk about your business convincingly and your aesthetics are attractive, you'll be much more likely to attract customers, partners, and financing if you need it.

Do Cool Shit Branding Exercise

Here's an exercise that you can do to help you clarify and create your brand. Answer these questions (*WILD* answers have been given below as examples), and once you do this, you will be well on your way to branding success!

WORDS

- **Mission statement:** The key to this question is not what you do, it is *why* do you do it?

WILD's mission statement: "Wild honors nature; the source of our uniqueness, our well-being, our future. It is a promise to choose ingredients that have been harvested with respect to their primitive state. It comes to us as it has come from the earth: already perfect. Please feast with confidence."

WHAT? HOW? WHY?

- What: What do you want to achieve or provide?

   WILD aims to provide farm-to-table pizza and local foods with a conscience to the locals.

- How: How do you achieve your goal?

   From the beginning, we focused on working with good local vendors: local farms, local breweries, local vineyards, local packaging companies, local furniture designers, and fair-trade coffee and tea companies. And now our messaging is evolving to put that message front and center. (We also made the bold move to serve exclusively gluten-free crust. We are confident in our crust as we spent a very long time perfecting it and tweaking it to what it is today.)

- Why: Why do you want to do this? Why is it important to you (or the world)?

   We aim to make America's favorite comfort food good for you and guilt-free, and we want to support local farms and suppliers at the same time and offer this favorite comfort food to everyone, even those with food sensitivities.

You will see that when you ask yourself these questions throughout the life of your business, your answers may very well change. It's an iterative process, so let that be okay with you.

VISUALS
- Logo: Decide whether you want just a word (called a word-mark), icon (a symbol), or mix of both.
- Colors: Select the colors of an existing company that you like and edit them slightly for yourself. Choosing two to three colors is standard.
- Font: Serif or sans serif—depending on your brand look and feel, your font will want to match the style.

You will feel *so* much stronger about your business if you can clearly answer these questions and make these decisions. If you do have the ability to bring on a branding agency that you trust, it's certainly a valuable proposition.

Don't settle for the first design you see. You are the one who has to live with this brand day in, day out. Radha worked with five different artists before she found the right one for her company, Super Sprowtz (supersprowtz.com), and now her logo is phenomenal and effective. I went through four branding agencies before I got my newest brand look and feel (thank you, Zach Lynd!). Don't settle until it's right!

LOCATION, LOCATION, LOCATION!

After I felt good about my brand, I moved on to the next phase: finding a location. I hired a commercial real estate broker. Interesting fact: landlords for some commercial spaces oftentimes pay the broker fees, so do your research and you might be able to get one for free.

The search took a while. Any good space that came up was getting gobbled up by franchises like Starbucks and Dunkin' Donuts because they were proven concepts and landlords liked to know that they would have a stable tenant in place for several years. Finally, after four months, my broker managed to find me a $6,000-per-month space on the Upper East Side. It certainly wasn't my first choice of location (I was hoping for East Village or West Village), but nothing close to those neighborhoods was available in the price range I wanted and one that I could actually win against proven concepts. The Upper East Side space fulfilled my budgetary stipulation, and it was on a main avenue, which was my other stipulation.

The main issue was that this space had previously been a nail salon. It was painted *pink*, had no basement, and wasn't designed for a restaurant. This was probably why no Starbucks or Dunkin' Donuts was going for it.

I would have to put in full venting (expensive ductwork to exhaust the ovens) and a hood, and dig out the entire basement to put plumbing and drains in the floor. It was a serious ordeal. I wasn't sure if $180,000 was going to cut it.

But I decided to go ahead with it anyway. I had been searching for a while now, and I had to get moving—otherwise, who knows, it could have been another four months of searching!

Thankfully, through my neighbor, I found my general contractor to build out the space. (You should always try to use word-of-mouth recommendations, especially if you are a first-timer).

DON'T LET THE PAPERWORK BECOME QUICKSAND

Once I crossed off the branding and real estate tasks, I had to attack the paperwork needed to open the business (this includes the permit to operate and tax documents). I didn't even know where to begin.

Sometimes the answer is incredibly simple. I called 311, the government hotline, and asked to speak with the business solutions department. I was shocked when someone picked up right away. The woman on the line said that she'd help me get everything I needed and was able to expedite the process because New York City had a new initiative to help businesses streamline the paperwork process. Nice! She said that she would help get every single department involved at the same time with my case so that there would be no delays in getting the business up and running. Well OK then! Why couldn't all government departments act with this much empathy and goodwill?

I made damn sure to let this helpful angel of a lady know that I was grateful to have her help and told her to please come to my restaurant for some free pizza next time she was in the neighborhood.

As this part of the adventure came to a close, all my paperwork was filled out and filed, thanks to my friends and one kind stranger at the New York City business center.

Do Cool Shit Takeaway

When all else fails, call 311 in your town and ask for the business solutions department.

You will still have to go and file the paperwork yourself (think DMV at every department), but at least you have someone holding your hand through the process.

Dealing with the city government is never fun and is one of the big things that keeps people from opening businesses at all, but just power through, stay patient, and find the nice lady in the business department who will help you.

Do Cool Shit Fast

If you'd like to tap into some available resources for starting your business, here are some quick and dirty steps to creating the basics of your business in a week:

• To get a domain name: godaddy.com or networksolutions.com

- To get a cheaply (and often expertly) designed name, logo, brand for your business: behance.com, crowdspring.com, 99designs.com, SVA.edu

- To get business cards made so you can hand them out to everyone you meet and start spreading the word: us.moo .com, gotprint.com, vistaprint.com

- To launch a quick website/holding page in ten minutes and start building your contact list: launchrock.com

- To create an effective blog and social media pages to build a readership and brand loyalty: wordpress.com, blogspot .com, tumblr.com, Twitter, Facebook

- To test your product to assess market share via local fairs or online stores: etsy.com or preorder sites like kick starter.com

10

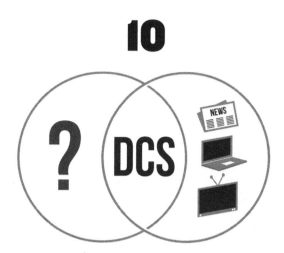

BREAKING NEWS

How to Get Media Without Knowing Anyone

If you don't like the news, go out and make some of your own.
—WES NISKER

A booming voice shouted at me: "Excuse me! You can't go in there!"
I kept walking as if I didn't hear him.

"Hello?"

Luckily, the security guard didn't get up from behind his desk. He cared enough to shout at me but not enough to actually chase me down. Everything was going according to plan.

As he continued to yell, I was still pretending to be on my cell phone, and me and my crisp-lined pantsuit (yep, one of the leftovers from the banking days) continued to zip right past him. I had my hair pulled back, and I felt I could be cast in the part of a young business journalist (Lois Lane—the ethnic version). I was so glad I thought of the cell phone move at the last minute. I quickly turned the corner, getting out of his visual range, and ducked into an elevator that was just closing. I was in.

The New York Times Building was *big*. I had one more front desk checkpoint to get past (what was this, the Pentagon?), but it was so important to get through. I needed to convince a *Times* food writer—any *Times* food writer—to accept my package and, hopefully, to write about my new restaurant. So what if I didn't really have an appointment with—er—any of them?

Game on.

It was September 2005 and my restaurant was being built on the Upper East Side. In the meantime, I had put together a map of the city that included every single newspaper, magazine, television station—anywhere and everywhere that could possibly feature the restaurant in their New Openings or Food sections. I put together a list of my favorites: the *New York Times*, *Time Out New York*, *Daily Candy*, the Food Network, the *New York Post*, *New York* magazine, ABC, NBC, *Food & Wine*, and a few others.

I thought about what could possibly make them want to write about an unknown, first-time restaurateur? I wasn't a chef, I wasn't a TV personality, I was just little old me. I would have to get creative.

I created a press release for my grand opening and made it sound as exciting as I could. I remember Rich Wolf had worked with a PR firm on his press release, so I used his as a model. I used phrases like *exclusive opening* and *intimate event*. I sent the letters to the addresses I found online, crossed my fingers, said a prayer . . . and waited. This was a different proposition than inviting people to a brainstorming session.

My response rate was a big fat doughnut.

I suppose the press wasn't clamoring to get an invitation to the "exclusive opening" of a pizza shop. It seemed that unless the Kardashians were showing up, the media didn't really care. What could I do that would make them care?

Wait, what if I showed up and delivered an invitation to these people at the press houses myself? Maybe then I would get a better success rate. It would be rude to reject someone in person, especially if I'm smiling and holding a boxed offering of freshly baked pizza . . . right?

It made me think of one evening when I was still working at the bank and finally spending my first weekend at home after working twelve consecutive weekends. (Yes, the math you just did in your head is correct. That's three months without a single day off.) As I walked toward my couch to zone out and enjoy the simple things that sustained me, such as my grilled salmon, sautéed veggies, and reruns of *Seinfeld*, I saw a note slide into my mail slot and fall on my floor. For the most part, I loved having a mail slot and not having to walk to a mailbox, but there were those few times when I slipped on my mail and almost fell on my ass, which certainly is not fun when you walk in, late at night, possibly a little tipsy from an evening out.

I picked up the note. I was especially curious as it looked like something I'd receive from a friend. I looked outside my window to see who brought it and nobody was within visible distance. The note was handwritten. It read:

Hi, Neighbor!

We are pleased to let you know that our place is finally open for the neighborhood to enjoy! Please come in with this note and try any appetizer on us. We look forward to meeting our friends around the corner and we can't be more thrilled to be here. Enclosed is our menu.

Best,
Susan and Dave
Owners of Café Around the Corner

I remembered thinking how cute this was. It was so sincere, personal and homemade, and it made me want to give them my business.

Now was the time to use this idea. I called Richard to help me come up with a really creative package to deliver to the media. I didn't want to create the standard press kit, which basically consisted of a folder with a bunch of boring papers inside that talked about the new business. It clearly hadn't worked when I sent the press release and invitation the first time.

I wanted to create something different. Something memorable.

Together we decided that we needed to have something with a bit more shock value because mom-and-pop restaurants were cute and all, but they didn't get reviewed in the *New York Times*. No, we needed something totally different and entirely weird to get the big guns behind us.

We threw out a bunch of ideas. I thought that sending the press kit in a nondescript box would be cool and intriguing. Richard thought maybe we should tell people to not eat anything until our place opened. No idea was too weird.

We both went home to think about our ideas. Richard called me a couple of days later, excited to share what he and his smart branding buddies came up with over a few pints of lager. "What if we created a nondescript brown box that you would then hand deliver to each press outlet? In the box, we would have a note that read in neat, old-school typewritten letters: 'The perfect food will be arriving shortly. Until then, don't eat anything.'

"And below the note, put an IV bag in it, like one from the hospital. And let's make stickers to stick onto the IV bags that read: 'Should the lack of sustenance prove to be debilitating, please insert tube into vein.'"

(Wow, totally weird. And memorable!)

"And then beneath the IV bag, we'd put the menu and opening-day invite. This box will make people stop what they are doing and at the very least tell their friends about it."

I thought it was totally brilliant.

I had a giant sign printed on white paper that said in big bold letters, "The perfect food will be arriving shortly. Until then, don't eat anything," and hung it in the window of my future restaurant. Within

Do Cool Shit Takeaway

If you have a list of things to do/people to talk to that seems daunting, start with the easiest ones first. It gets you warmed up, but also in the case of talking to people, early successes can boost confidence so you're in great form when you get to the harder "asks."

Also, the one connection that you have can lead to other great connections as well, so always ask if they have favorite bloggers and writers who they may recommend to you.

minutes, people started coming over and taking photos of it. It was working! I was getting buzz!

I called one of my friends whose dad was a doctor, and he offered to give me fifty IV bags. They arrived at my doorstep one week later.

Next, I bought fifty craft brown boxes and printed the notes and menus to add to the box. I printed out a New York City map, penned in every location I needed to sneak into, and with my bike tires freshly pumped and the boxes assembled and secured in my bike basket and balanced on my handlebars, I took off.

What could have been a successful adventure turned into a mini-disaster because within three seconds, the bags on my handlebars hit my front wheel and jammed into it, which kept it from moving forward. As physics was now the star of the show, I flew directly over my bike handlebars and landed in a heap on the street.

Thank goodness that I'd learned the ole tuck-and-roll move back in elementary school. I popped up as fast as I could (c'mon, I was an athlete too), brushed myself off, sheepishly collected all of my boxes that had flown everywhere, turned around, and immediately headed back home.

I tended to my bleeding palms (and bruised ego) and decided that all was *not* lost—I just needed to reduce my load, slow down, and change my strategy a bit. I decided to make my first stop at *Daily Candy*. It was the only press house where I had a connection—I had a friend in common with the editor. I figured I'd start there to warm myself up (especially needed while nursing that bruised ego), then be better prepared to walk in cold to all of the other places.

Daily Candy was located downtown Manhattan. I got back on my bike, and a short while later, bandaged palms and all, I walked in as confidently as I could and approached the front desk.

"Hi, I am here to meet with Pavia." Pavia was at that time the editor in chief of *Daily Candy*.

"Do you have an appointment?"

"No, but we have a friend, Anne, in common."

The secretary looked at me and my beaming smile and said, "Ah, OK, let me check."

She picked up her phone. I held my breath. My face started turning red, I could feel it. (Blushing is the worst. It's like a big old sign to everyone saying, "I'm nervous!" Ugh.)

"She's busy but she said she'll come out to say a quick hi."

I clutched the brown box tightly and waited. I started sweating. What if she thought this IV bag idea was terrible? What if she was annoyed that someone without an appointment was bothering her? I brushed those thoughts aside and concentrated really hard on what I was going to say.

Pavia walked out a few minutes later and quizzically looked at me. "Hi," she said.

I greeted her with my warmest smile. I said, "Hi, Pavia! My name is Miki and my friend Anne has been telling me forever that you and I need to meet."

She smiled, so I continued.

"Anyway, I wanted to actually invite you to our grand opening of my new healthy, farm-to-table pizza place on the Upper East Side! We have gluten-free and vegan options as well! Here is the invitation for it."

I handed her the box.

She took it but didn't open it (thank goodness), smiled, and said, "Aw, well that's nice of you to stop by. I'll certainly look on my calendar to see if I have an opening that night. Thanks so much for the invitation." I decided not to ask her outright if she would write about us and hoped that the package would give her the nudge she needed.

I thanked her, gave her a hug, and watched her take the box back to her desk. I hurried out before she could open it.

With my confidence boosted that one person at least took the box, I decided to go big. Next stop: Florence Fabricant (affectionately known as Flo Fab) at the *New York Times*.

She was one of their most seasoned restaurant critics and if she wrote about the restaurant, it would be a massive boost for my business. I hoped that since she was a woman who had obviously taken her career very seriously, she might empathize with me and my dream. I told myself that it would be a victory if I could just get the box to her, even if I didn't get a chance to meet her (and become her best friend. OK, getting ahead of myself).

Before walking into the New York Times Building, I stood outside and pretended to be on my cell phone, while looking in through the glass. I wanted to study the movements of the people walking in and out of the security area.

After feeling like I got the rhythm down of how the guard would let one visitor in and call the next person in line waiting, while no longer paying attention to the door, I took a deep breath and started walking toward the turnstiles. As the little doorway was closing, I caught it in time and slipped right in.

I was still pretending to be on the phone when I heard the guard yell at me to stop. I kept my phone to my ear, kept walking as fast as I could, and ducked into an elevator that was just closing.

After a few long, deep breaths to soothe what felt like a heart attack, I pretended to look frustrated like I couldn't find an address and asked the other people in the elevator if they knew where the food editorial department was. I got the answer I needed and hit the button to that floor.

When I got off the elevator, I saw a secretary sitting at the front desk. She was older and she looked *fierce*. There was no way I could avoid her. I walked up and told her that I had a package for Florence Fabricant. I asked if I could speak with her.

In a monotone, yet sharp and direct voice, she said, "She's not here and packages should go through the mail room. I'll take it this one time."

"Are you sure she'll get it?" I asked.

She looked up at me with annoyed eyes and bitingly said, "Yes, she'll get it, but you'll be more certain that she'll get it if you go through the mail room at the service entrance like everyone else."

She took the box and dismissed me.

Although happy that my box was on its way, my mind started to race. Wait, service entrance? Mail room? All I had to do was put the name of the writer or editor who would be receiving the package and it would 100 percent get to their desks? Well, that made my life much easier! At least if I got reneged at the door, I'd have a backup plan that would work.

Immediately following this experience, I went to all of the other newspapers, magazines, and press houses with a *lot* less fear, and if I got turned away at the door, or failed in my attempts to get to the intended recipient, I just went to their mail rooms to drop off the rest of my weird boxes. At every stop, I made sure to chat up the mail clerks—after all, I never knew when I'd have to come back! In the end, I hit up fifty places in five days, going back and forth from my apartment with four to five boxes at a time, and although I saw mostly mail rooms, I also got to physically talk with four writers, which was unexpected.

Once the packages were dropped off, all I could do was wait and see what happened. While I waited, I printed out five thousand copies of my menu and wrote a note to my neighbors (similar to what I received in my mail slot), and photocopied the note on a special card stock paper to make it look like I wrote each one by hand.

Rather than sending them through the mail and having them sit there among the Banana Republic catalogs and utility bills, I spent the next week going from building to building (starting from my restaurant

and moving north, south, east, and west systematically), waiting for
someone to come out of the buildings, then sneaking in and leaving a
flyer on the door of every apartment. I knew I could have hired a flyer
service to do it, but I wanted to do it myself to make sure that it got done
properly and that the letters were sitting on top of the doorknobs and
not slid under the door. It was important to separate my note from the
rest of the mail noise. I was excited to see if this effort would translate
into actual sales.

Do Cool Shit Note

**Note how important it is at this critical juncture (right at the be-
ginning) to do everything you can do yourself, to ensure that the
job is done right and for the least amount of money (especially
if you are on a shoestring budget like I was), and that it's done
exactly the way you want it done.**

It was Wednesday, November 9, when I opened up the *New York
Times* dining section and I. Freaked. Out.

There I was, holding one of my signature rectangular pizzas with my
consulting chef, Tomas, and an article written by Flo Fab herself! I had
no idea that she had gone to my place to actually try the food. The *New
York Times* had asked to come in and take a few shots without promising
that there would actually be a piece in the paper. But there it was, in
print, for all to read. PIZZAS FOR ALL, BE THEY DUNCES OR GENIUSES (We
used to call our plain cheese pizza the Dunce and our build-your-own
pizzas the Genius.)

I ran straight to the corner store and bought ten copies. You better
believe it that my grandparents in India were getting a copy.

In addition to that review, *Daily Candy* wrote a dedicated article
about us, *Time Out New York* called us the "Upper Crust of NY," and
a segment aired on Taxi TV via NBC (the little screens in the back

of taxis in New York City). All told, my little pizza place was written up by more than fifteen different media outlets in the first year of opening.

I will also mention that 95 percent of my delivery sales that first week came from the note I hand delivered to every apartment in the neighborhood. My tiny, little 450-square-foot healthy pizza shop was officially on the map!

HOW TO GET PRESS WITHOUT KNOWING ANYONE

Here are some straightforward suggestions to help you attract media attention for your new passion project.

STEP 1: Print out a map and pinpoint every media outlet in your city and neighborhood that you are targeting.

Collect as much information as you can on each place—company, address, general phone number, hotline phone number (where you call in for story ideas), e-mail addresses, names of editors and writers, etc.

STEP 2: Call as many media outlets (or press houses, same thing) as you can.

There is generally a phone number to call to pitch story ideas. If you can, always call instead of e-mail, especially in this day and age. People can hide behind e-mails and not respond, but they will have to talk with you if they pick up the phone.

What you say when you do get someone on the phone is crucial, as you usually only get one shot at it. Try this:

Hi! I'm calling in from [name of your company]. I wanted to ask you a couple of quick questions, as I have a really exciting new story to share.

Since I want to make sure this story is relevant to you and not to waste your time, what kind of stories are you looking to publish right now? A personal piece, goodwill piece, entrepreneurship piece, political piece?

This way, you are starting by engaging them in a question and *not* pitching them right away. Also, since everyone likes to feel like an expert, generally they will offer advice if you ask for it. In this case, the advice may help you make your pitch back to them even better!

Sometimes, they may not be open to sharing what they're looking for, but many times they are. The whole point of having a hotline in the first place is for them to get good ideas! The warmer and more confident you sound, the more likely they will answer. If they spell out what they are looking for, all you need to do is create a story that ties into your project.

Then the next question you can ask:

What are some of your most successful stories from this past year and why? What was it about them that made them successful?

This is an important question because (a) you're still engaging them by asking them questions, and (b) if they answer it, you can tailor your story to be even more appealing to them.

Thank the person and get off the phone. Now you've got the information you need. You don't need to reinvent the wheel, you simply have to find out what worked in the past and how you can be what they are looking for.

STEP 3: Create something original and/or weird and/or funny for writers to want to write about, using the knowledge you gained.

Stay away from writing a long press release, because chances are, nobody is going to read more than the first sentence or two (if you're lucky). Remember, people think in short sound bites now (just think about Twitter's 140-character limit or how often you read a Facebook status all the way to the end when it's longer than a few sentences).

Know your audience. If you know that one editor is more serious than another, try to tailor the package and your delivery to match his or her personality. Otherwise, make it weird enough for everyone to like it. They'll "get it" in the way they choose to, right?

Do Cool Shit Attention-Grabbing Methods

Create a unique and engaging video that introduces you and your business to the press. You can easily use iMovie to edit a short video and the quality is excellent. Deliver the video in a creative way. For example: Put the video on a little external pen drive that you can gift to the writers and editors along with a note. If these editors and writers don't want to download a video from someone they don't know, you can give them a DVD that is also creatively packaged with handmade touches.

Create your own box with something weird—like what we did with the IV bags—or with something useful and repurposed inside that is relevant to what you are trying to do. Packages are always fun to receive, and it will make your idea stand out from the many others they hear about every day. You can find weird things to buy at dollar stores and thrift stores and places like Film Biz Recycling (filmbizrecylcing.org), where they repurpose things from film sets instead of throwing them in landfills. Put your items in a box along with your invitation, catalog, or menu.

Always have an ask. Make sure that whatever method you use, you state clearly and concisely what you are asking of them: to come to your opening or launch and/or to set up a meeting or call with them.

STEP 4: Personally hand deliver your own press packages.

It will save you money (every parcel delivered in Manhattan by a bike messenger costs about twenty-four dollars), and it is a way to meet the writers and editors when you are dropping the packages off. Great opportunities always arise when you put yourself in the position to have these opportunities.

STEP 5: If you do meet one of the writers or editors, after you hand them the package, give them a hug!

It will completely throw them off guard and sometimes disarm them into actually being friendly and open to what you have to share. (Obviously, use your own judgment here. If the person looks really grumpy or angry, maybe stick with the firm handshake and a big smile! But choose to go in for a hug if you can!)

STEP 6: Try to get an e-mail address to follow up.

Following up is critical in closing the deal. Sometimes writers and editors get really busy and even if they liked you, they may be bogged down by their own deadlines and very distracted, so a gentle nudge the day after you meet them or deliver the goods can be really helpful. And if you don't hear from them still, follow up a week later. And then every two weeks until you finally hear back. Unless they tell you otherwise, continue to follow up with them. Persistence pays off!

A great way to remember to follow up is to use the free Gmail plug-in called Boomerang. Its function is to bring your sent message back to the top of your in-box so you don't forget to follow up.

Gmail has another great plug-in called Canned Responses (go to your Gmail settings and you will find the plug-in). If you are pitching the same thing over and over again to many different people, rather than having to copy and paste the same message continuously, you can simply click on CANNED RESPONSES and it will automatically put in the text you want in the body of the e-mail. It will make follow-up and sales calls so much easier!

STEP 7: Write a cute note (sign it yourself!) and flyer all apartments in your neighborhood.

Explain your business idea sincerely and why it's an MB product for the customer. Do everything it takes for people to get to know you and want to root for you. It worked for that cute café a long time ago and it will work for you too!

The most important thing to remember is to keep going! Don't stop pushing when you raise the money, and definitely don't stop pushing when your doors open or when you launch your product—that's when so many people quit, but that's only the beginning!

Getting people to learn about your concept and fall in love with it is a challenge, especially if you can't afford to hire a PR company. But you *can* do it yourself, you just have to be tenacious and wake up every morning with the plan to get people to know about what you're doing.

11

DISASTER LAUNCH

How to Win Back First-Time Believers
After Big Mistakes

Only those who risk going too far can possibly find out how far one can go.
—T. S. Eliot

I could feel my breath quicken and a tightening sensation build in my throat. The voice on the other line shouted, "I am never ever ordering from you again! And I'll make sure my friends don't either."

Before I could respond, I heard a click.

Wow.

I checked the other orders. They were backed up by more than an hour and a half. I glanced at my overwhelmed workers, who were doing the best they could but were still so new to this job that I couldn't blame them. I had hired the pizza makers only the week before and they were not prepared for such a big rush right away.

The phone was ringing off the hook. Every time I picked it up, it was another person calling to complain that their delivery was late.

I took a deep breath and tried to calm myself down. This was so much harder than I thought. At this point, all I could do was put my head down, keep going, and get the customers their food as fast as possible.

How in the hell was I going to get through this one?

My parents always said that "there is a time for everything." There is a time to study, a time to play, a time for dinner, a time to clean the house, a time to meet someone, a time to get married, a time to have kids, and a time to become a doctor (my parents never stopped hoping).

When my friends or I would go through tough breakups, we would often say to one another, "It just wasn't the right timing for you guys." When one of us interviewed for a job we were excited about and didn't get it, we'd say, "The timing wasn't right. Maybe a better job is just around the corner."

It probably wasn't a surprise to anyone that I ultimately became an entrepreneur because I've always much preferred to march to the beat of my own drum and take charge of my own time. I would show up to social gatherings late, I would usually be the last one arriving for meetings (oops!), and I never cared too much that my parents wanted me to be married by twenty-six and have a child by thirty. I just did my own thing.

So, as though the gods of time were keeping score and accumulating bad karma for my lack of respect for time, it all came down *hard* when I opened my first business.

It was one of the most difficult lessons I've ever had to learn.

I was advised by Rich Wolf to have a "soft opening" before trying to get press to cover my restaurant. I would quietly open my doors and iron out the kinks for a few weeks and allow my new staff to learn their jobs and get comfortable in the day-to-day operations. It was the time to receive initial feedback from customers and fix any issues that came up. Once everything was pretty much ready, we would have a grand opening and scream from the rooftops that we were open for business.

But I was so excited about getting the press interested in covering my little pizza shop that I didn't heed Rich's advice and delivered my press boxes earlier than I should have.

The first big article came out in *Daily Candy* a couple of weeks before I opened. When it was published, I was high-fiving myself, sending a link to everyone I knew, happy that the restaurant was featured in a noteworthy online media outlet. The little idea in my head was actually a newsworthy article? I was proud and beyond thrilled.

What happened next was far from thrilling; it was more like a horror film.

When I got to the restaurant on the very first day we opened our doors, about fifty people lined up outside, excited to taste "the perfect food." Wide-eyed and a bit incredulous, I hurried in to my restaurant to get it ready as my phone was already ringing off the hook and I had a dozen voice messages from people asking when we would be open.

Really? *Daily Candy* was this powerful?

This was the original location of the restaurant on the Upper East Side of Manhattan, and unlike our current one in the West Village, it was set up as mostly counter service where people would walk up, place their order, and either sit down to get the food brought to them or wait to take it out. We only had eight tables in the place and we weren't set up for delivery yet. We had hired the last of our staff the day before, and while most were hired about two weeks prior, they didn't really get any training until the week before we opened, since we had still been waiting on some equipment to come in.

The night before our opening, we prepped eight trays of pizza dough (which was about sixty-four pie crusts), we had the fresh, home-made marinara sauce ready, our organic mozzarella grated, and the toppings sautéed and ready to go. Since it was our first day, we had no idea how much to prepare, so we put together only a couple of two-quart buckets of each ingredient. According to our consulting chef, that should have been enough to get us through the first week. But we weren't considering what would happen if the press we'd been hoping for actually worked.

I felt unprepared. It was like I was a kid playing grown-up and all of a sudden, I had lots of other people playing the game with me. It was weird and surreal that people were lining up to buy something from my new business. It hadn't even really sunk in yet that I even had a real business.

The more pressing problem was that I was completely clueless as to how to handle this mess. I never dealt with customers in a restaurant before. This was going to be a big learning curve for me, and unfortunately this would cost me some of my customers.

I felt better that Chef was with me to set everything up and train the new staff, but even he was overwhelmed by the turnout on the first day. Neither of us had thought to prepare for this scenario.

The process was incredibly bumpy on our first go-round. Aside from the normal first-day problems, like getting the hang of taking orders and filling them quickly, and learning how to use the new cash register, and making the pizzas from scratch, we also faced logistical and layout issues. Our to-go bags, paper plates, and napkins were two steps beyond reach of the employees, adding too many wasted seconds to the process. Our assembly line wasn't perfect (for example, the sauce and cheese were placed on the wrong side of the toppings), which added precious minutes to the process, and the distance from pizza prep table to the oven was too wide, resulting in a few burned elbows and arms as we tried to place the pizza into the 650-degree oven. *Owwwwww!*

It felt like our entire staff was walking waist-deep in snow, trudging uphill with a heavy load on our backs. All we could do was keep going and pray it would end soon without something horrible happening. The whole experience was truly painful. And the customers weren't having any of it.

At first, the line of customers seemed to only keep growing, but after a while, many people in the back of the line grew frustrated and left, some of the customers who already paid and were waiting asked for their money back, and those who did manage to get their pizzas, got them so late, that they were grumbling and most likely walked away with imperfect (and cold!) pizza. In our attempt to move things along, we may have pulled the pizzas out of the oven a little too early and we all knew that if the food wasn't good, they wouldn't come back. The whole thing was an epic disaster.

Once we finally closed our doors to the public that night, our team came together and we talked about all of the things that went wrong and tried to celebrate the few token things that went right. We moved the plates and napkins so they were within reach of the cash register. We moved the sauce and cheese to the left side of the toppings so the assembly line flowed properly; we prepped a lot more food so we didn't have to worry about running out; we went over the cash register details again. One by one, we went down the list of bottlenecks. We spent the rest of the night soothing our wounds (both figuratively and literally!) and tried to get as prepared as we could.

The next day and then the following two weeks went gradually better and better, but that *Daily Candy* article really did its job and we still had so many people coming in, we felt as though we were trying to mostly keep pace in this game of frightening catch-up instead of feeling as if we were in the lead and strong. If only I had listened to Rich and that article had been written two weeks later, we'd have been in much better shape.

This was certainly not the way we wanted to start—a thousand steps behind. But one thing was for sure: I would never underestimate the power of a good review again.

I knew for sure that we lost a lot of customers in the first two weeks. People had sworn to us that they would never come back and that they would tell their friends about their bad experience with us. Comments like these stung, and when they were written online, the sting lasted even longer. I came to learn that making mistakes like this was part of the learning process and the only thing to do at that point is to pick yourself up, fix what was wrong, and move forward as fast as possible.

. . . .

Needless to say, the entire first month we were open was rough. Once the *Daily Candy* article hype was over (and before the big Food Network show was coming out in January) the dust settled and I found myself with the opposite problem—slow traffic coming into the restaurant during Christmastime.

Ninety-five percent of restaurants close in their first year, and many times within the first six months of operation. And usually it's because the restaurant doesn't deliver on its promise. Either the food, service, atmosphere, or the overall execution doesn't work. Most people will not try the same place twice if their first experience wasn't positive. Unless you're family or a close friend, you will not give the business the time to figure things out and get it right. This is why having a soft opening was so critical! Rich's advice finally made sense to me but now it was too late.

My back was already against the wall financially. How did this happen so quickly? I had just started! WTF?! I had two options. Either I could throw in the towel after all this work and be one of the 95 percent that doesn't make it, or I could fight and win back the customers who had sworn us off.

I thought about my parents and the time they took out a loan when we were kids in order to take the family to India and Japan to visit our families and teach us about our heritage. It took my parents many years to pay back that loan, but to this day, they agree that it was money well spent and they would do it all over again.

Years later, my parents also made the tough decision to send all three of us to Ivy League schools, again going into debt but feeling that there was nothing more important than a great education to get started in life. My four years spent at Cornell were so important to my growth as an individual and my experience there changed my life in ways that still affect me every day. I owe my parents a lot and admire them so much for their willingness to fight for something that we grew to believe in just as much as they did.

I knew I couldn't give up on my little place. It would be a hard fight, but I knew that the effort would be worth it. I knew that I would learn a lot about myself and how to strengthen my backbone amid a tough, humbling challenge.

With this renewed clarity and purpose, I pondered what to do first. We had to fix all of our issues, including those with training and food preparation. Everyone learned how to expeditiously take orders on the phone or in the store, and we hired proper delivery guys. Through it all, we grew more cohesive as a team and even started to have a little fun.

Once we ironed out all of the issues, we were ready to spread the word and encourage more people to visit. I knew I needed to make significant moves to win back our customers' trust. To make a golf analogy, I was asking for a mulligan. I needed a second chance.

Honesty always being the best policy, I handwrote another letter, but this time it was different. It said:

Dear Friendly Neighbor,

We are finally ready to reintroduce you to the tastiest, healthiest pizza you've ever had. We've worked hard to get to this point, and we are looking forward to sharing the improved version of ourselves with you! We support local farms and local suppliers and we are excited to talk with you about where the food you're eating comes from. We think you will be pleased!

  Do come in with this note and have your first slice on us.

All the best,
Miki and the SLICE Family

I then printed five thousand copies on quality parchment-like card stock and spent the next two days signing and folding them by hand one at a time.

The following week, I snuck into every building in the neighborhood again and flyered every single apartment. I knew that some of these people never tried the food at my restaurant and may have been confused by the note, but I figured that it would intrigue them enough to come and check it out. Everyone wants to be part of an underdog story.

I probably could have hired someone to flyer for me but, again, it was important to me that it got done properly. I was also willing to take the risk of being caught loitering, and since I don't look very suspicious, I knew doing it myself would give me the best shot at a successful guerilla marketing campaign quickly. Eventually, I had to learn to trust my staff because I simply could not do it all, but in those early stages, it was all me.

The only run-in I had was from one of the fancier doormen buildings in the neighborhood who caught me and stopped me after I flyered two floors. I explained to that doorman that I just opened and would love to invite him to my spot and dine on the house, and he was more forgiving thereafter.

Once I got done with flyering (it took about three days, morning to night), I moved on to the next thing.

I needed a way to win back a group of people all at once, rather than having to actually win them back one by one. I thought about all of the places in the neighborhood where I might find potential customers. Healthy pizza would appeal to those who lead a healthy lifestyle. Gyms, playgrounds, yoga studios, schools, and office buildings would be a great place to start.

I headed to the gyms first, with the goal of making the experience MB always in the back of my mind. I approached the gym manager and said, "Hi, I would love to offer a free sample of my pizza for your guests. It's healthy, tasty, and I think they would find this a nice perk after their workout." I quickly explained my business to him. He said, "No solicitations, thanks." Not fazed, I took a weekend course in Pennsylvania and got my spin instructor's license to teach at gyms. Now, on the inside, it would be much easier! And it was.

The manager practically rolled out the red carpet for me, giving me the best spot in the gym to sample my pizzas for three days and allowing me to promote my business by putting flyers in the locker rooms and at the front desk for a whole week. Wow, what a break! Now he was excited because he thought it might entice new members to join. He too understood the magical power of free food. I was excited as I imagined just how many people I would reach this way as well.

I stopped by every other gym within a ten-block radius and secured tastings at every single one using the same MB technique as before. I locked in fifteen evening tastings over the next three weeks at pretty much every gym in the neighborhood. This was going to help a lot.

Next stop: local playgrounds.

First I took the time to observe the parents, who would usually just sit there on the bench watching their kids play and either read a magazine or fiddle with their cell phones. It was the perfect opportunity to go and talk with them about a new healthy place for their kids to eat. I showed up every sunny day for a week around two thirty in the afternoon and sampled the pizzas and handed out flyers. Some of them mentioned that they had gone once and had a bad experience, but most offered to come back now that things improved. It's amazing how far free food and a personal touch can go.

I moved on to yoga studios and office buildings, and within one week, it all started paying off! The phone began to ring and people starting coming in again, and business grew—little by little, person by person. It had worked! My business was officially back on track.

Do Cool Shit Lessons

- As much as you can, try not to make your customers be a part of your learning curve. They won't be willing to let you catch up and fix mistakes. It's a harsh reality that all they will remember is that their experience wasn't great. As much as you can, wow them from the start!

- Have a soft opening first. Quietly open your business and work out the kinks with friends and family over a couple of weeks. When you "go live" with real customers, do it slowly, and once you feel like it's flowing well, then you can have your grand opening. Consider a soft opening as a dress rehearsal, where you can get your lines down before the big night.

- Set up free tasting nights for neighbors or a free product test for the locals. That will ensure that people will come in to try it out and, in exchange, will give you valuable feedback for their experience. This will enable you to adjust and make changes as comments come in. These free nights are MB for both parties—guests get free food and you get free and real feedback.

- Time it with the press that the opening day will be two to four weeks after you actually open quietly. It can take several months of lead time before an article will get written sometimes, so plan ahead as best as you can.

- Figure out where your customer base lives, works, and spends their leisure time. Approach them with an MB idea. Offering a free perk is always a great way to open a door.

- As part of the soft opening, create an event where you offer free tastings or trials to draw your customers in and start a word-of-mouth campaign.

- If you make mistakes the first time around, do everything you can to deliver properly the second time. Otherwise, you're going to have to do it all over again and your customers may not be as forgiving the third time!

- Honesty is the best policy. Especially in today's climate and economy, your customers are highly suspicious of being duped or taken. Admitting to your mistakes and offering honest and concrete ways in which you are fixing them will make your customers much more forgiving, and is more likely to bring them back for a second try.

- Don't take no for an answer. There's always a way in.

- Business is iterative. Nothing is ever absolutely perfect, and it often takes much longer than you'd expect for a business to get on its feet. It's OK. Just keep improving. Never stay stagnant. The minute you do, that's when the business stops. No matter what, celebrate the little things that go right, even if the rest doesn't go according to plan. You have to celebrate the positives so that you and the team can stay motivated!

12

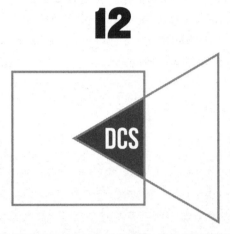

PARTNERS IN CRIME

How to Find the Perfect Business Partner

Life is meant to be shared.

—*Into the Wild*

She said it in a matter-of-fact, dismissive way that unnerved me and made me want to reach through the phone and shake her.

"We ran out of dough, so I have to close the restaurant down at six p.m. today. Sorry."

"Wait, what? How on earth did we run out of dough? We're a pizza place! We can't run out of dough!"

"I have no idea, but I don't know what to do from here and I think we need to close."

"No, we can't close! Please figure it out!" It was a weekend and one of our busiest nights. We count on weekend business to make back some of the slower weekday business.

"I don't know what to do. I'm out of ideas." Click.

She hung up on me. *What?*

I was still three hours away in upstate New York, checking out a local farm from which we were hoping to source some of our ingredients, and I couldn't get to my restaurant to solve this big problem. My general manager had completely dropped the ball.

How did I get in this position, with a manager who clearly didn't have good problem-solving skills and who clearly didn't understand the restaurant business? But of most immediate concern, how was I going to get out of this jam?

I've always had a partner in crime: my identical twin sister, Radha. And my dad's nickname for her—Rocky—perfectly sums up her personality (Rocky refers to Rocky Marciano, the American heavyweight boxing champion). Let's just say she lives up to the qualities her nickname suggests. You don't want her as your opponent.

Rads managed to squeeze into the world and take her first few breaths five minutes before I did. She came out kicking and screaming—and with jaundice. I came out next—breech. Interesting way to enter the world—one yellow and the other butt first. Our parents knew from the get-go that we'd be a handful.

We were also born a month and half premature and weighing only five pounds each. We were teeny tiny. My dad used to be able to hold one of us in each of his open palms.

Now, while this could have predicted a difficult journey for some, the story goes that we were supposed to be incubated at the hospital for six weeks but practically drank the hospital out of milk, put on pounds very quickly, and were discharged within a week. It seems our fighting spirit came right along with us at the time of our birth.

Our older sister, Yuri, was born only eleven months before we were, so the three of us grew up doing everything together. My parents would dress us alike, we were all part of a twin club in Montreal (Yuri was allowed in too, since there was less than a year between our ages), played soccer on the same team growing up, and went to the same schools at the same time.

Throughout the course of our lives, we had to learn how to share, how to take ownership of our own things, and how to compete with each other in many areas—including boys and sports. So often, Radha and I would end up playing against each other in the finals of badminton tournaments (think Serena versus Venus with a birdie). It was hard because we were always on the same team in an "us against the world" kind of way, and to have to face each other in battle was so strange. Not to mention the annoying refrain of "You're just mad because I won" coming from the backseat of the car after those competitions.

As for dating, we both won, lost, and kissed some of the same boys throughout the years, but we never let a boy come between us. We stuck to the "I saw him first" rule, and while it could be frustrating, it saved us both a lot of heartache.

Slowly over time, Yuri separated herself from us and started to gain her own identity and make her own friends. Radha and I continued to do everything together. When Yuri left to go to Harvard, we decided for the first time not to follow her. We chose to go to Cornell instead.

Rads and I roomed together in college every single year except for when we studied abroad, and once we graduated, we lived together in New York for our first five years. Anytime either one of us had a boyfriend, he soon learned that he basically had two girlfriends to deal with most of the time.

We did try to learn about personal space, even if Radha and I were sharing a physical space for most of our childhood and adolescent years. We learned how to be individuals and part of a collective but that only really happened years later, just in time for us to start our own (separate) businesses. Regardless, our twin partnership saying will forever be: "From the womb to the tomb."

When I started my business, I had to start thinking in terms of a different kind of partner—an actual business partner. I initially looked for someone who was like my other partner, my sister. I hired a person who was like me: young, excited, educated, hungry to build something . . . with no real regard for their level of experience. I had done it, so they should be able to do it!

I figured that I was smart enough to step in and figure things out if my manager didn't know how to do something. I figured wrong. No matter how smart my partner and I were, it wouldn't help us serve customers faster or manage a new staff of twelve people when neither one of us had ever managed anyone before.

For the first few years of my business, it often felt like the blind leading the blind. There was the former coworker who was fun, smart, and dedicated, but who had no experience at all. There was the know-it-all who also had no experience. (A know-it-all who doesn't know it all is the worst!) Then there was the culinary institute graduate who had experience in the restaurant business but whose true dream was to be a chef, so I lost her as well. I finally learned that what I needed was someone who was equally excited about making the business grow but who was much more experienced than I was.

Looking back, I would have spent more time raising money so I could hire someone experienced rather than go through years of messing up and starting over again and again with different people. Don't make my mistake! Spend the time and money up front to get it right the first time. Choosing your business partner is one of the most crucial decisions you will ever make.

So back to that Sunday afternoon on what will forever be known as the Day the Pizza Place Ran Out of Pizza.

I asked my manager why we were out of dough. She said that it was a weekend and that no purveyors were dropping off supplies and she had forgotten to check inventory on Thursday for a Friday delivery. Since the ordering wasn't done early enough, she missed the delivery cutoff time on Friday. She said that even if the dough was delivered on Sunday, it wouldn't be ready on time for dinner service.

The only solution she could think of was to close the place. Since she couldn't or didn't want to think of a creative solution, it was up to me. I told her to go to the neighborhood pizzerias and buy enough dough from them to last through dinner.

To my surprise, she said, "No, I'm not doing that."

When I asked her why, she said, "Because it would be humiliating." She sounded defeated.

"What would be more humiliating would be to close a pizza place down on a weekend because we have no dough."

She refused to do it.

I was stuck. In the end, I called my kick-ass friend Kosta, an entrepreneur who started several businesses himself and knows what it means to be resourceful, and asked him to go around to neighborhood pizza places and borrow dough from them. Within thirty minutes, he had brought back fifty units of dough and I had personally called around from upstate and got another twenty-five units of dough available for pickup.

It became clear that I needed someone experienced and fast. It's wrong until it's right. You just never know how things are going to play out.

Do Cool Shit Lesson

Hire slow, fire fast. I can't stress that enough. No one has ever said that they fired somebody too soon.

Always check references. This is so important in the hiring process. There must be at least three working references and they must all check out. It may take time, but as with the last piece of advice, it's worth it to take your time and get it right from the start.

When you call references, ask these four questions:

- **Did the candidate ever do something extraordinary without being asked? If so, what?**

- **How would you describe the way people react/interact with the candidate?**
- **Why aren't you working together now?**
- **Would you hire him or her again?**

Even if you have experience in the industry in which you're working, make sure your partner does too. Another option is to approach people who have experience and offer them a small salary, plus equity in the company.

Your business is going to take up a significant portion of your life. If you sense that your partner does not share your values or vision, don't be afraid to cut them loose. They will drag down your business, energy, and excitement, and in the end your business will suffer.

I understand that it's hard to let go of this partner because you don't want to be left alone to pick up the pieces, but the sooner you do it, the sooner you can move past it.

You may be daunted by the prospect of starting over, but trust me, it's like tearing off a bandage; it's terrifying at first, but it only stings for a little while and when you find the right person for the role you need to fill, things will get exponentially better.

ON PARTNERSHIP

There are some important questions you should ask yourself when contemplating a partnership. I break it down into two categories: business characteristics and personal characteristics.

Business Characteristics

- Do you have a shared vision—do you both envision the same future for your concept?

- Can you learn and be challenged by this person?
- Do you have different complementary skill sets? What does he or she bring to the table that you don't have?
- Will he or she have your back no matter what? Even through fights, do you have confidence that he or she will never screw you over?
- It's important to debate, to have passionate discourse. It means that both parties *care*. You don't have to agree on every single detail and should argue why your idea is important, as long as the overall vision is a shared vision.
- If you find yourself disagreeing with the way someone carries him- or herself, approaches business, or treats people, you are fighting an uphill battle. You can address specific actions and events, but the odds of you fundamentally changing someone's behavior are slim.

Personal Characteristics

- Laughter is essential anytime, anywhere. Is your partner able to put things in perspective and cut the tension with a little humor or silliness?
- Do I admire the other person? Admiration in both friendship and business are so important. Generally you admire someone who can do something better than you or can do something that you simply can't. Have different skill sets. And vice versa. The mutual admiration is *key*.
- Is he or she curious? Is this someone who is constantly interested in learning about your industry, constantly striving for more, discovering best practices, and simply finding new ways to kick ass in business and life?
- Do I generally like the other person? Would I be OK sitting next to this person on a twelve-hour flight?
- Is he or she resourceful? You want someone who willingly takes on challenges that don't have set instruction manuals, someone who solves problems without a set path in place.

Once you find your partner and find yourself hiring new employees, make sure they feel their voice is heard and valued. Your partner will feel validated if they are contributing to the growth and identity of your organization.

If you are bringing on a managing partner, let them help you lead the hiring for the rest of your team. Trust that they will want the best workers to work for them and it will also create a clear line of protocol between you and the employees. The employees will deal with the manager and the manager will deal with you. All of a sudden, you went from dealing with dozens of workers to one or two managers. It will free up your time to think more about the bigger picture and the growth of your company.

If you think that your manager has skills that you don't have, has staying power, and will continue to make the company better, *incentivize them* to stay by making them an equity partner and grow with equity and profit sharing.

Hiring the wrong management person or team can completely stunt the growth of your business. I had to dig myself out of a hole several different times because of lack of experience and poor management skills, and if I simply had someone who had a positive attitude and who understood the fundamentals of a business, it would have exponentially sped up the business's learning curve to success. Hiring incorrectly did help me go through the "hazing" process of starting my own business, so I do feel stronger because of it, but I would definitely have chosen the easier route if I knew better by hiring the best person right off the bat.

There are some very simple things you can do to make sure you've found your perfect match. Take your time, do it right, and reap the benefits.

I finally have two *great* partners right now, one with forty-four years of experience in the restaurant business, John Arena, who owns the popular pizza chain Metro Pizza in Las Vegas surrounding areas. He is encouraging, positive, fun to work with, and *knows* this business inside and out. He is also a karate instructor on Saturdays, so he has a real Zen sensei quality about him. My other partner is Tony Hsieh, of course, whom I gain so much inspiration from pretty much all the time. I feel blessed and ready to tackle the next stage of this company!

13

SUPERSPROWTZ.COM

DOING GOOD AND DOING WELL

How Can I Follow My Dream and Still Fix the World?

From what we get we can make a living; what we give however, makes a life.

—ARTHUR ASHE

The super what?" the six-year-old boy asked while he was visiting the restaurant with his family, looking at one of the colorful books that he'd picked up off the shelf.

"The Super Sprowtz!" I said.

"Who are they?" he asked excitedly.

"They're a gang of superhero vegetable characters who keep us safe against the bad guys like Pompous Pollution and his evil henchmen!"

He leaned in, excited to learn more about these new superheroes. "Really? What are their names?"

"Well, my favorite is definitely Colby Carrot."

"Why?"

"His super power is super sight! He can see things far, far away and has laser vision, even better than Superman!"

Nick's eyes widened. "Really?"

"Oh yes! So when you eat carrots like Colby Carrot over here, then you can get super sight too! Do you want super sight?"

"Yes!!" He ran over to where his parents were, grabbed a carrot out of his dad's salad and stuffed it in his mouth, and exclaimed, "I'm going to get super sight!"

His parents were shocked. His dad came up to me and said, "That is the first vegetable my son has ever eaten raw in his entire life. How did you do that?"

"Superpowers," I said, "will get you everywhere." I handed him a Super Sprowtz book with a smile, and as I walked away, I thought of how wonderful it was that children could be encouraged to be healthy like this.

The power of the imagination, I tell ya.

I always knew that I wanted to do something beyond simply starting a successful (and growing) small business. Building more locations and having the opportunity to franchise my business is exciting and all, but I knew that I could get even more satisfaction from helping my community.

As usual, when confronted with a problem, I thought of my parents. My mother is a Buddhist and my father is a Hindu, so we grew up with plenty of Siddhartha and Gandhi stories. We learned about the value of helping others early on.

My mother started the Gifted Children's Summer Camp in 1989 to keep excelling students engaged and exploring their creativity. She couldn't find a good educational summer camp in our area, so she simply started one herself. With no experience (sound familiar? The apple doesn't fall far from the tree!), and with English as her second language, she just figured it out as she went along and the camp existed for years with hundreds of kids and very grateful parents.

A couple of years later, my parents started "Tomorrow's Professionals," an educational electronics company that made fun kits to teach kids about electronics. This was the early '90s and it had become clear that computers and electronics were going to be huge in the future. My dad wrote the manual, and my mom assembled the kits and drew the artwork. I still have two of these kits as mementos (and will one day sell them as vintage kits for hipster kids), and I can't help but feel a little tickle of pride and amazement every time I come across them. My mom spent time teaching inner-city kids how to use these electronics kits, so they too could excel in this new and growing field. It was always so fascinating to watch my parents create little enterprises for the good of society.

I don't know if the term existed back in the '80s and '90s but these businesses that my parents created were the classic examples of *social enterprises*. Today, there seems to be a clear zeitgeist around the way people view social impact. Having positive influence in the world has officially become "cool." Young people are getting behind movements (think Change.org), caring about the environment (think the Leonardo DiCaprio film *The 11th Hour*), and gay tolerance (think Macklemore's song "Same Love"), and are looking to innovate and change things in their local communities for the better.

Another perfect example is Tony Hsieh. After selling Zappos.com to Amazon for more than a billion dollars, his new purpose became to create a real community in downtown Las Vegas, an area that never really had a sense of community before. Las Vegas had been known to be a tourist destination, which made it difficult for large communities to flourish.

His goal became to change that.

His dream is to create a place that is a mix between the best aspects of New York City, Silicon Valley, Burning Man, and South by Southwest. He wanted to help facilitate serendipitous encounters, which is one of the things that makes New York City so special. New York City has a huge population in a small amount of space, and whenever you go out, you have the opportunity to run into more people, thus creating a tight-knit community. In Las Vegas, the houses are quite spread out, and part of Tony's mission was to build taller, affordable housing in downtown Las Vegas and to invest in local small businesses so that a real sense of community can be built.

He is now well on the way with this project and has recruited and invested in one hundred businesses already to grow their roots in down-town Las Vegas, and in 2013 is even moving the Zappos.com employees from the suburbs to City Hall, the building he is renting as the new headquarters for the company. He now talks more than just about ROI (return on investment) when he makes an investment; he more often talks about ROC—return on community. How will your idea have a direct impact on the community? I love that.

President Clinton said the same thing. In December 2010, I managed to get myself invited to the Clinton Global Initiative (CGI), where leaders from around the world would unite to create and implement innovative solutions to the world's most pressing challenges. CGI has successfully improved the lives of 400 million people in more than 180 countries so far. Not too shabby. The way they ensure quick turnaround for change is to have individuals and organizations make annual pledges to hit positive impact benchmarks. These pledges keep people motivated and excited to come back the following year to share their positive impact stories.

For example, a pledge could be for a company to build all their new constructions with solar panels. Another pledge could be for a company to help buy clean syringes for underprivileged community hospitals. Or to give away one thousand pairs of shoes. It can be big or small, it doesn't matter. As long as positive change is being achieved.

President Clinton consistently speaks about "doing good and doing well." To create a financially successful business that has underlying good for the community built into the business model is the way of the future.

This concept of "social entrepreneurship" kept reappearing and con-tinued to resonate with me.

I started to think about my own business using the lens of "doing good and doing well." My restaurant was definitely built with the same intention: to create a pizza that both tasted good and was good for you, and also supported as many local businesses as possible.

We worked with local produce and dairy farmers, local microbreweries, local vineyards, fair-trade coffee and tea companies, and even worked with a local packaging company. In this way, we not only were helping employ thousands of local jobs and supporting the local economy, we were getting food onto people's plates that had higher nutrition content because of the short transportation times as well as playing a part in helping the environment by cutting down our use of fuel and cross-country (or even farther!) packaging materials and costs.

Still, I knew we could do more. I wanted to engage and educate our clients, especially the future leaders of the world: our kids!

The obesity pandemic is growing, and obesity has become an issue of national importance. At the restaurant, Rads and I noticed that kids never ate vegetables on their pizzas and that they pretty much stuck to plain cheese pizza with its naturally limited amount of tomato sauce. They never ate salads or our vegetable appetizers. We knew that there had to be a way to help the parents in their quest to get their kids to eat healthier.

Radha took on this challenge like a champ.

We knew that we needed to create something different that would engage kids about healthy eating in a fun way, so we brainstormed and thought about all of our favorite childhood playthings.

Our first dolls were Skippy, a cute little chipmunk doll, and Ganzy, a little bear doll. Rads and I would play with Skippy and Ganzy all day long and create long stories and adventures with them. We then recalled our other favorite toys: Transformers and Care Bears, and our favorite movies were Superman and Batman installments. There were two common themes here—superheroes and adventures!

What better way to educate kids than through superheroes going on adventures? So Rads began to create a really fun coloring book on the inside of our restaurant menus and kids would come to the restaurant and color in the menus and learn about why the different vegetables were good for them (without knowing that they were learning, of course), and we let their imaginations run wild while they waited for their pizzas to arrive.

It was really great to watch these little superhero characters change the way the kids thought of vegetables. It actually worked! Kids would run and order broccoli because they wanted to be super strong like the character Brian Broccoli, or they would order eggplant because they wanted to be super smart like Erica Eggplant.

The kids ordered (and ate!) more vegetable toppings and ate more greens than ever before. The parents were ecstatic.

So we (mainly Radha) took this idea that was clearly working and over the next three years built a 2.0 version of a classic children's show like *Sesame Street* complete with puppets and stories that focused on food and nutrition. Since the Super Sprowtz was born, she has published four children's books; produced a live puppet show that has been performed for more than a hundred thousand kids; and created a TV show and produced a series of a dozen PSAs with celebrities including Russell Simmons, Shaquille O'Neal, and Aasif Mandvi from *The Daily Show with Jon Stewart*. She even has a permanent exhibit at the Children's Museum of Manhattan! Check out supersprowtz.com, and you will fall in love with Colby Carrot, guaranteed.

Do Cool Shit Takeaway

Here's a simple method that people can use and one that many of my successful entrepreneur friends have employed to create "social enterprises."

Ask yourself these three questions:

- What is a problem that you are passionate about that's negatively affecting your life or the lives of others in your community or other communities?

- What is an idea or a solution that could alleviate the strain of this problem?
- What is a product, service, or business you could create that could make this solution possible?

My responses that led me to create *my restaurant*:

- My belly was hurting all the time. I was passionate about food. I found out that it was because food was becoming more and more processed and full of antibiotics, hormones, and pesticides, and this process was affecting millions of people around the world (including me). And like 65 percent of the population who suffer from a reduced ability to digest lactose without knowing, I was also lactose intolerant and didn't know it.
- To create a place that offered food (pizza!) that was free of processed ingredients.
- We are a farm-to-table pizza concept where people could be entertained and eat their favorite comfort food without guilt.

Here are Radha's responses that led her to create Super Sprowtz:

- Childhood obesity is a big problem in America, and parents needed a fun way to teach their kids about veggies and to show them it's "cool" to eat healthily.
- To create a fun way to teach kids about nutrition, health, and eating more vegetables.

- **Super Sprowtz is an entertaining adventure series about veggie superheroes who save the planet one veggie at a time. Through books, live puppet shows, a TV show, an educational curriculum, and museum exhibits, children everywhere are inspired to eat better and lead healthier lives.**

WHY PEER PRESSURE CAN BE AWESOME

When you're hosting an event, whether it's for your own business or for your passion project to help your community, the most important thing is to make sure the invited guests promise out loud and in front of the others that they will create specific tangible impact goals. Saying it out loud will help that individual keep to their goals.

Create follow-up events (six months and one year later) and celebrate the success stories of those *who have* achieved their goals and show those who didn't that it's easier than they thought to make a difference.

There's nothing like a bit of peer pressure to get people doing good work. Ultimately, everyone wants to be heard and have the ability to share success stories. Sharing positive stories within communities gets people even more excited to do good work and it creates an upward spiral effect.

THE CALL TO ACTION

Create a double-bottom-line business around solving a societal and/or community problem in conjunction with being a financially profitable company. This will reap the most rewards overall.

Look around you—there are so many problems to solve, it's just about your taking notice and deciding to take action! If you feel the calling within your heart to be part of this movement, go start a social enterprise and tell me about it on docoolshit.org!

. . . .

So! You just learned a lot about what it takes to get yourself started to begin your dream journey in business and create lasting impact. In order to continue to kick ass in business and follow your passion at full throttle, having a fulfilling and healthy personal life will give you important perspective in your life, which will actually enable you to make better business decisions in the long term. You will have time to step back, recharge, spend time with your friends and loved ones, and take yourself outside of what you are doing workwise and get outside the box. It has been incredibly important to me to have a personal life because it actually fuels my business life too.

So these next chapters are meant to remind you that staying healthy, finding love, and building your community are equally, if not more, important to your overall happiness as is your life's work.

14

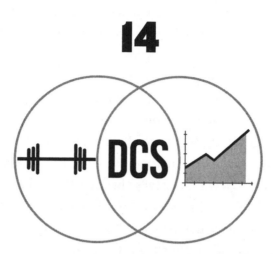

KEEPING IT TIGHT

How to Take Care of Yourself While Running Your Business

The greatest wealth is health.

—Virgil

'm *so* busy, I can barely stay afloat. I have no time to think about anything else!"

"I travel all the time. It's hard to get into a rhythm!"

"I'm not a morning person and by the time I get home from work, I'm exhausted."

"I've gotten to the point of no return. It would take a miracle for me to lose this much weight."

I could go on and on and on listing the excuses people give not to work out and eat better, but keeping it tight when you're busy with work is not rocket science.

You may be looking for an easy answer, like wearing more Spanx, but at some point, your clothes are going to come off.

How many books and blogs have been written about this? Probably tens of thousands, and the problem with many of them is that they contain way too much detailed and unnecessary information, intimidating readers. It's just about the fundamentals!

Let's solve this issue right here, right now. I will tell you the simple and practical things I do and show you how I've helped so many of my friends get to their ideal weight, stay healthy, and do it all while working the sometimes crazy hours it takes to keep their businesses successful.

Case in point: Mary. I met Mary through Rads. She worked in publishing and was always sitting at her desk working and leading a very sedentary life. Mary had tried diet books, trainers, starvation—and nothing worked. She would start off strong and would fall off. She was so frustrated, she finally gave up. She knew I was able to stay healthy and work out, even though I had a crazy work and social life. She asked me how I did it, and this is what I told her.

Most people know about the two important components to staying in shape: diet and exercise. And, yes, those are the two key components, but there is a third *most* important one:

MENTAL REFRAME

Mental reframing means thinking of diet and exercise in a new way.

Reframe the word *diet* and use the word *power* instead. How are you powering your body up? What will make your body power itself up better?

Reframe the word *exercise* and use the word *release* instead. Working out is amazing; it releases endorphins in your brain, which are natural uppers. It allows you to work things out in your mind from the days' happenings and clears your head meditatively. Moving your body releases stress and tension and is the best way to improve your mood. Moving and releasing your body of stress actually gives you *more* energy, even if you work a twelve-hour day. It's counterintuitive, but it's true!

More than anything else, being physically fit is a confidence booster, there is no makeup or outfit or costume that will make you feel better about yourself than feeling good under your clothes. Working out will improve your perception of yourself.

OK! Let's dig into the *how*. It's not that complicated, I promise.

Let's start with *power*, the bigger challenge for most people. Within power, there's the food and drink. Let's attack drink first.

Reframe in your mind that nothing will quench your thirst more than a glass of water, no matter where you are.

Your goal should be to replace *all* drinks with water. Everything. No more juices (juices have empty calories and are very high in sugar—if you want juice, eat an orange or apple) and no more sodas, even diet sodas (those are worse for other reasons than calories, and in some cases, have been linked to some types of cancer).

Let's do the math real quick.

A can of soda, a juice, a bottle of beer, or a glass of wine is approximately 150 calories. If you drink two drinks in a day, you're at 300 calories: 300 calories × 7 days/week is 2,100 calories. So by drinking only two little (in your mind, harmless) drinks per day, you're ingesting an entire extra day's worth of calories. Don't do it!

So if you simply replace these drinks with water, all of a sudden you're dropping a TON of calories, and weight will just start falling right off, it's incredible. And, your thirst will be quenched.

If you are ordering alcohol at a party, order vodka and soda (not tonic, which is full of sugar) or vodka water; that has minimal calories and you can flavor it with a lime twist.

That's it!

That's my drink secret. It's so basic and it works. It's *up to you* to reframe this in your mind!

Drinking = Quenching thirst.

Try it for sixty days and see what happens to you. Come and post on docoolshit.org about your experience.

Now, on to food:

This is the important power that gives you energy to continue to work on your business with as much energy and pep in your step. Pick what you put inside you wisely!

My mental reframe came from an interview I saw featuring Natalie Portman.

She said: "I feel powerful when I choose *not* to eat something bad. It's a true test in willpower."

I live in New York City. I barely have time to cook. I've been lucky enough to date guys who have been amazing cooks, so I've never really had to cook. Opening a restaurant has been great because I can get fed there too!

My point is: I eat out almost all the time and most of my friends do too. It's New York City after all!

Here are my simple tips to keeping it tight when you eat out.

When you order a meal, simply try and order the healthiest item on the menu. Choose fish over red meat as much as possible, and choose greens over potatoes most of the time. You know where it is on the menu. Have the will to choose that kind of nourishing power to give you the most energy possible.

Next, *share your entrée* with someone.

Rads and I still share most of our meals. In fact, when we lived in Brooklyn together for five years, we used to do Dinner and a Movie Twin Date Night, where we'd go to see a new movie that was released at the local cinema and eat dinner at our favorite Thai place. On Tuesdays, new releases were only five dollars and at the Thai place, a big plate of pad thai was only ten dollars with tip and tax. So we had a full, fabulous dinner and a movie for ten dollars each. It was the best ever.

If you are alone or want to order your own meal (or if you are feeling the peer pressure to order your own meal), eat half of it for dinner and save the other half for lunch the next day. When your meal comes, *split it in half* right away and eat only the left side. It's a game and you will win!

Two things happen: you save money *and* you eat half the calories. You win twice!

Do Cool Shit Takeaway

Let peer pressure work in your favor.

If everyone at the table is ordering their own meal, ask, "Does anyone want to get beach-ready and share a meal with me?" Most likely someone else will want to be beach-ready too.

Next, chew your food twenty times. Breathe between bites. Allow your stomach to catch up to your hungry brain. It usually takes fifteen to twenty minutes for this to happen, so slow down your eating. (I know, it's hard for me too, that's why I started chewing a lot more per bite and it really helps a lot. Chewing a lot also really helps with digestion.)

Just don't spoil your appetite with bread and chips. I love bread and chips at restaurants; it's so hard to not eat them. If you work out an hour or more every day (and are at your ideal weight already), then go for it in moderation, but otherwise, stick to a salad starter and eat half your entrée. If you really like bread, eat half of a small slice or piece and savor each bite!

Try not to eat dessert, but if you must eat dessert (like I do most of the time), share one!

Literally, that's it! That's my eating-out secret. No big deal, right?

The rest of the day when you are not out, try and eat small little meals. I know it's hard to remember to pack snacks, but eating a healthy breakfast and having small snacks all day is the way to go. Then have your half dinner.

Here are some of the options I go to in the morning and for snacks:

MORNING

- soy yogurt with fruit, spoonful of granola and spoonful of nuts
- banana and a smoothie or fresh juice
- egg whites with spinach (if you have more time for breakfast)
- cereal with rice milk and fresh berries

SNACKS AND LUNCH

- carrots and hummus
- apples and all-natural peanut butter
- nut mix
- popcorn with sea salt and no butter
- small salad with a few veggies, scoop of tuna salad, and sesame ginger dressing

Quenching your thirst and powering your body properly will make all the difference in how much energy you will have throughout your day to keep up with work and have energy and libido in your social life.

Do it and *no* excuses!!!

Now on to releasing (remember, the reframed word for exercise). Think about your time working out not as something new to add to your agenda but as an activity that is rewarding and fulfilling and re-places another less rewarding commitment in nature.

The best example is watching TV. TV is a time suck, and it really doesn't improve your life. It just doesn't. It may be hard to get rid of TV entirely, so try getting rid of cable first, if you have it. I've been without cable TV for the past four years and it has changed my life! I only watch movies on my television set. You have no idea how much time you waste vegging out in front of the television when you can be doing other, more productive things, like working out at the gym or outdoors or in a dance class or at the climbing wall or whatever!

I am all about unwinding and relaxing, but watching TV is just not the answer!

Here is how I mentally reframed myself to be able to hit the gym every day and make it not feel like a chore.

The first thing is that working out generally puts me in a new environment. I get to see new people and sometimes make new friends. Working out can not only relieve stress, but it can also be an engaging experience.

The second is: build romance into your workout experience.

My friend and confidant Zach loves to work out because he gets to experience the sunset every evening as he skateboards to the gym. It makes going to the gym so pleasurable for him. He experiences that dreamed about "New York moment" whenever he goes to the gym. Find your "New York moment" to get you out the door and in your running shoes!

The third is: sweating is fun.

Think about most of the fun times you have sweat: on the beach, out dancing, having sex, riding your bicycle with friends—so much fun happens when you sweat. Always use that as a motivator to get you going.

Matthew McConaughey's workout mantra is "Sweat every day, no matter what," and I think he's onto something. As long as you sweat in some way every day, that will jump-start your metabolism and you will see your body start to transform.

If you don't like going to a gym (sometimes I like to work out at home), that's OK too, you just have to find your thing. You can do a cross-fit workout like me. All you really need is a mat and a couple of dumbbells.

Here is my workout (see the workouts in detail on docoolshit.org). It's mostly resistance training (using my body weight to work out) and some small weights. All you need is a mat and some dumbbells and a medicine ball.

I do these in a row and then repeat three times with a one-minute break in between. You must keep your heart rate up!

- Pushups × 20
- Lunges × 25, holding 10-pound dumbbells
- 3 arm workouts (biceps/triceps/shoulders) × 25 with 5-pound dumbbells
- Sit-ups × 50
- Squat with medicine ball toss × 25
- Mountain climbers × 25
- Jumping jacks × 25
- Stretching for 15 minutes at the end

Here is the best motivator to get you going: find a partner! Having a partner does a couple of key things:

- It holds you accountable!
- It helps establish relationships with those you want in your life. Maybe it's a person you want to connect with in the office, a new friend you want to get to know, someone you have a crush on, etc. It's a great way to not have to get drunk together, but get to know people the wholesome way!

Ultimately, the power lies in your hands. If you want to find power in your own willpower, it will change the way you look on the outside and how you feel on the inside. The better you feel in your skin, the better the chances that your real, most authentic self will surface.

15

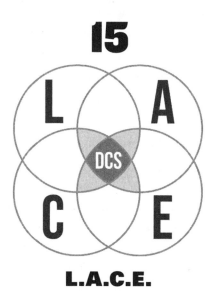

L.A.C.E.

or, How to Teach Men a Thing or Two

There is never a time or place for true love. It happens accidentally, in a heartbeat, in a single flashing, throbbing moment.
—Sarah Dessen

Burning Man, 2011

Miki! I need your help! I don't know what costume to wear!"

My friend Andrew and I were looking around the big costume tent at Kostume Kult, a well-known camp at Burning Man. We were among a hundred other people rummaging through racks and racks of costumes, and we were captivated by the wild array of colorful and creative items.

We definitely needed to find new outfits. Andrew was wearing this horrible poncho, and I was determined to find something sexier for him to wear. It reminded me of a potato sack, and it covered his whole body— which I knew from previous events was quite hot!

The cool thing about Kostume Kult is that while the costumes are free to take, you have to put yours on and walk out onto a runway in front of hundreds of spectators on your way out.

As I rummaged through one of the boxes, I found a gold pharaoh neck ornament, a pharaoh crown, and golden arm band. We found a white sheet and tied it around Andrew's waist. The poncho came off and the gold jewelry was placed on his bare chest and bulging bicep. I fastened the crown on his head.

"OK, I think you're ready for the runway." I smiled and hurried out of the tent so I could take a seat by the runway and watch him walk out in his new and improved getup.

The master of ceremonies, a hilarious and long-gray-haired man with nothing but a short girly tutu on and no underwear was calling out the next runway models.

"Next, we have a Pharaoh King with his princess!"

Mediterranean music was cued and one of the Kostume Kult girls danced out first in a sexy tasseled bikini top and tasseled skirt, carrying a ceramic bowl over her head. As Andrew walked in behind her, back straight with perfect posture and his strong bare upper body with the gold jewelry shining in the sunlight, I had to gasp. As he danced with the girl, he eyed her up and down seductively and did a playful turn.

My jaw literally dropped as I watched him strut behind her and dance for her (and for the audience). I'd never really looked at him in this way before. It was in that moment that I fell in love with him.

We had arrived at Burning Man the day before, new to this incredible experience in the Nevada desert where sixty thousand people gather for one week to experience the engaging surroundings and people in the midst of incredible art and music.

We arrived at Burning Man as friends, but little did we know, we wouldn't end up leaving that way.

Rewind six months:

Andrew and I first met at Summit at Sea. I would like to say that there was instant attraction when we met, but it took a while for it to get to that point. We met on the dance floor, rocking out to the Roots and Pretty Lights under the stars, somewhere in the middle of the Atlantic Ocean. Nothing *happened* on the boat, but we knew there was something there between us. He lived in Washington, DC, at the time anyway, and long-distance was out of the question in my mind.

Over the course of the next six months, I saw him twice—both times I was dating other guys. I had just gotten out of a three-year relationship and told myself that I would date freely for a year before jumping back into something serious. I've been known to be a serial monogamist, so I was giving myself some breathing room to date and have fun!

It was at my family's annual barbecue, Agra-Palooza, that we decided to lock in our plans to finally go to Burning Man together with my sister, a group of my close friends, and my then boyfriend. We ironed out the details, and we spent the next two months planning for this trip. We had to secure an RV, get flights, and get all of the food, bicycles, costumes, and gear to deal with the harsh desert climate.

Things were looking good, until about ten days before the trip, when shit hit the fan. Radha and her then boyfriend backed out last minute saying that they had too much work and not enough time to plan. Then the guy I was dating and I broke up.

That left just me and Andrew. We said screw it and decided to go for it.

The two of us flew into Reno on Thursday night, a day earlier than planned, because we wanted to escape from Hurricane Irene. We got a cheap hotel room for a couple of nights, and we even shared a bed but literally put pillows in the middle so that we could establish a clear friendship boundary.

During those two nights together, I learned more about him and it was great. He had a great attitude, carried himself like a natural leader, and seemed to always be happy and up for anything. Furthermore, he asked so many thoughtful questions, and I noticed that he was a great listener. It felt good being with him and about to head out on this awesome adventure!

The first day at Burning Man was a blur. It was like being on Mars. We couldn't believe the kind of art that was set up all over the desert and it was one discovery after another of breathtaking new art and installations created by inspired and inspiring artists. The music was some of the most inviting, infectious, happy, exciting, body-moving stuff I'd ever heard. It was just a phenomenal thing to watch sixty thousand people peacefully experience a festival like this. I was again really impressed with Andrew because his bike pedal broke the first day (the Burning Man grounds are vast and everyone had to get bikes) and he had to use his foot to push the bike forward, which was a giant pain in the ass in the desert, but he never complained once and just struggled with a smile.

Nevertheless, Andrew and I explored and danced the whole first day. It was the second day that really changed everything.

After the runway moment at Kostume Kult, where he was transformed into a pharaoh, I knew I wanted to be with him. I already loved dancing with him (being a good dancer is a big draw for me); I loved the way he walked and carried himself; I loved how he listened, and I loved that he was highly empathetic. Instead of going to work at a flashy and high-paying hospitality job when he was twenty-two years old, he started a nonprofit called Dreams for Kids DC, which helps at-risk youth with career and life skills. I was smitten.

We went on a great adventure together all over the Playa (what they call the Burning Man grounds), and I was hoping to spend all night hanging out with him as well.

But then he told me that he didn't want to.

Huh?

That threw me for a loop. He asked me if he could go on a night adventure with some of the boys and he didn't want to include me. I was really bummed out but pretended like it was no big deal, and I decided to go an adventure with my dear friend Alex.

Alex and I ran around all over the Playa from dance party to dance party and had an absolute blast, but all I could think about was Andrew. I worried that he was off meeting other women.

It was 5:00 a.m. when Alex and I finally headed back to our camp and I popped by Andrew's tent to see if he was still out. I was sure he wouldn't be, but when I peeked in, I was ecstatic to see him there, asleep.

I must have been delirious and I don't know what came over me, but I crawled into his tent and I leaned over and quickly kissed him on the lips. As soon as I kissed him, he screamed and I jumped up; I said, "Oh my god, I am so sorry! I don't know what I was thinking." But he calmed me down and said, "Sorry, I didn't know who it was. Why don't you come and lie down?" Sheepishly, I went to bed next to him on his blow-up mattress and snuggled in for the night.

The next morning, I escaped his tent before he could wake and went to get breakfast at the camp's headquarters. He came and found me about thirty minutes later. I was still really embarrassed from the night before but put on a brave face.

I said to him: "Hey, I'm sorry about last night, not sure what I was thinking."

He paused and said, "Miki, I think you're the coolest girl I've ever met"—(flattery will get you everywhere!)—"but I'm about to move to Chicago and start a new life there. Not to mention, I really want to keep you in my life as a friend and I just don't want to screw it up. Does that make sense?"

I responded softly, "But it's Burning Man . . . Who cares, no? There are no rules here. Can we not overthink this? If I want to kiss you, maybe just let me? And if you want to kiss me, go for it."

He paused and said, "You're right," and smiled.

That day, we went on another great adventure—checking out new art, attending some seminars—and that night, as we were dancing under the stars, we finally really kissed for the first time. It was a deep, passionate, and wonderful kiss, and I was so happy in that moment.

The next morning, I again snuck away from Andrew—this time I left for an entirely different purpose. I went to his tent, where I spent the next few hours cleaning and tarping it properly, and then I took his bike with the still broken pedal to one of the camp mechanics to get it fixed. I had never been more excited to lend service for someone. When Andrew woke up and came to his tent, he found me there, cleaning next to his newly fixed bike. He grabbed me and kissed me.

We were both so giddy from that point forward. I think we were just so excited to have found each other in such a strange place. We wanted to celebrate finding each other on the Playa and looked inside the program book to see if there was somewhere we could go to celebrate and saw that there was a place called Wedlock Ranch, where someone named Reverend FunkPocket "married" people.

When we got to the ranch, we saw a man with a big, giant handlebar mustache, playing the ukulele, and asked him if he knew where Reverend FunkPocket was. He put his ukulele to the side and joyfully exclaimed, "Why, that's me!"

We decided to be married on the Pier to Nowhere, which is where Andrew and I watched the sun set for the past two nights, and it was definitely our favorite place within the festival grounds. It was a real pier, but since it was built in the desert, the artists put speakers underneath it playing sounds of waves crashing. They also secured fishing rods at the end of the pier where people could "fish for anything your heart desires." So brilliant!

Yay! I was getting married for the first time. (Since it was a Burning Man wedding, the marriage only lasted for one week, which was perfect.) I've heard it said that one Burning Man day is like three months in the real world. Where cell phones don't work and there are none of the typical distractions of life, we experienced more and discovered more about each other and about ourselves. With this kind of focus within and on the present moment, Burning Man was the place to reveal so many things and manifest it all.

I believe that loving someone is the most important experience in a lifetime. My mother's biggest (and only) lesson about lasting love: "Always maintain a little mystery." Make the other feel safe in your love, but keep them on their toes. What good advice. Thanks, Mama.

Andrew came up with an acronym that really resonated with both of us. It's LACE. We found that these were the four pillars of a successful, lasting relationship:

Looks—to be undeniably attracted to each other
Adventure—to bring new things into each other's lives; to want to try
    new things together
Challenge—to challenge each other mentally, physically, and spiritually
Enhance—probably the most important, to enhance each other's experi-
    ences wherever we go and whatever we do

As I watched the sun begin to sink, I realized I had only a few min-utes to get ready! I ran to my RV, found some sheer white fabric that I had purchased at Walmart, and some gold ribbon. How did I know that I would end up needing this fabric? The wise energies behind Burning Man just knew!

I made a sari out of the fabric and a white Lawrence of Arabia–style headdress with the gold ribbon, threw my boots on, and rushed out of the RV and onto my bicycle. I can still remember how my heart raced as I was speeding against the setting sun toward the pier, with my head-dress trailing in the wind behind me.

When I got to the pier, I threw my bike down on the ground and rushed up to get to the top where the ceremony was being held. We didn't know anybody attending except for the reverend. It was all random people spectating, which to me was even more whimsical and romantic.

As I was climbing up the pier, I tried to look for Andrew at the top— my bearded man wearing the plain white sheet around his waist—but as I looked through the crowd that was forming, I got only a glimpse of a gorgeous, clean-shaven man wearing a brand-new baby-blue seersucker suit with a beautiful red-and-blue handkerchief in his lapel pocket. Who was this person?!

I did a double take because I realized that it was Andrew!! I had *never* known him without a beard, and I had no idea where he could have gotten that suit. I couldn't stop staring at him. I was in awe; he looked incredible.

When he saw me, his face lit up and I could sense that he was just as excited to see me as I was with him.

Andrew and I held hands, and the truth was, words were exchanged but all I could do was grip his hands and stare at his beautiful face, including his handsome and newly exposed jawline and look deep into his sparkling eyes.

This was it. This was the love I had always dreamed of.

Since then, Andrew and I have traveled to twenty-seven cities, moved four times, and even got remarried at Burning Man this past year (in front of fifty of our friends, including Rads!). We are still happier than ever! You can check out the video at docoolshit.org.

We certainly have faced our set of challenges, but we are learning something about each other and about ourselves every single day.

Here are my love lessons I've learned thus far.

- Take three deep breaths when you feel like blood is rushing to your head and you are losing your patience. I can tell you that I used to be one of the most impatient people I know, but I realized that in order to communicate effectively, you need to take a step back and allow the other person time to understand where you're coming from.
- Stuff like "Can you please look into my eyes when I have a conversation with you?" "I love it when you compliment me," "You're touching me wrong," and everything in between may take a few times before he remembers and gets it. Be patient, and try and be cognizant of the things that your significant other wants of you.

  It's sort of like telling someone who has never spoken German to "speak German now!" and they're like, "But, but, I've never spoken German before!" and expecting that they will pick up the new language right away. You need to give him a chance to learn the new love language, especially if it's foreign to him.

- Listen sincerely. Sometimes it's important to just let him finish before you say your piece. Bite your tongue, take those three deep breaths, and actually listen sincerely to what he is saying. The more you listen, the better your understanding will be. It's so hard, I know, because your mind may be going too quickly and you often have an answer before he's finished. Do your best to let him finish. It will go a long way toward understanding each other and having a more intimate relationship!

- Do something nice for your partner often. Surprise him with gifts and experiences when you can. It doesn't have to cost anything— just create a memorable experience for the two of you to show that you are thinking about him.

- Be willing to grow together. You are not perfect. Your partner is not perfect. Remember that!

- When things are really heavy and the conversation is getting ugly, really try and cut it with a joke, or come up with a word that resets the situation. Andrew and I have the words *fresh start* as our key words to start over and reset the mood. It's all about keeping that promise to actually start over in your mind if you say that special word or words. It can be hard to do in the heat of the moment, but you can train yourself to do it.

- Give your partner space to do his own thing. Let your partner have space. Nobody wants to feel kept. If you prefer spending all of your time together, then that's awesome—but that's not everyone's thing.

16

STOP WITH THE SAME-OLD, SAME-OLD

How to Bring New Adventure and Travel into Your Life

There are so many doors to be opened, and I'm not afraid to look behind them.
—Elizabeth Taylor

When you get to Third Street, and you begin walking west from Third Avenue to Second, there will be a black door on the north side of the street. Knock three times and wait. A man who looks like he's about one hundred and fifty years old will open the door, and when he does, pretend like you know him—his memory is a bit like a sieve these days—and say, 'Hey, Frankie, it's me!' He will let you in, don't worry, and the place rocks. It's open for the most part from Thursday to Saturday night."

Black door? Knock three times? Old man named Frankie? I couldn't believe it. I'd been living in New York for eight years and never known about this speakeasy. Apparently it had been the hot spot for the mob to go since the 1930s, to grab a beer and chill without the 5-0 after them.

Radha and I couldn't wait to go. Our friend Matt told us about it, and he always knew about the coolest and most fun things around.

That Thursday, we beelined for the black door at around midnight. Sure enough, after knocking three times on the black door, an old guy opened the door, We said, "Hey, Frankie, it's me!" in unison, and sure enough, he let us in. Wow.

As we entered, it was as though we stepped back in time to the 1930s (à la Woody Allen's movie *Midnight in Paris*). The light was dim, there were rows of dusty photos of random Italian-looking men in hats and suits, an old dirty pool table, and some beat-up leather couches, and, of course, the bar. Behind the bar was a regular old white fridge, the kind normally found in someone's home kitchen, and one of those ancient cash registers that looked like it was from the 1800s.

We each ordered a beer, and the old guy behind the counter opened the fridge, took out two beers and said, "Beer is five dollars." When we handed him a twenty dollar bill, he put it in his pocket and said, "I have no change." He handed us the beers and walked away. Amazing. It was obviously part of the experience, and maybe a particular act of initiation for newcomers—and we delighted in it.

This same old guy behind the bar put a jazz record on a phonograph and then came over to regale us with the stories about the men in the photos. It was quite possibly the most authentic New York experience ever, and I was in heaven.

We could have gone anywhere else on Thursday night. But we decided to go out on a limb—in our own town. And now we have a cool story to tell because of it. I dare you to go find that weird place in your hometown, maybe even seek out something off the beaten track, and come away with a story to tell. And when you do, tell me about it at docoolshit.org.

Doing cool shit means you have to stop doing the same shit every week. It means committing yourself to doing new things and putting intent into your plans. That's all adventure is. New experiences. Different settings. Random encounters. That's why traveling is so much fun—because everything is new.

For example, when Rads and I graduated from Cornell, we bought a round-trip ticket to London and a Eurail pass that was good for two and a half months. That was it. We made no other plans. Sometimes planning an adventure means not planning anything at all, except for an eventual ticket home. The intent we had on that trip (and I can't recommend it enough) was to just go where the adventure took us.

When we arrived in London, we met up with my pals from my semester abroad and spent the night catching up at one of our favorite bars in South Kensington, where we all used to go together. We laughed about our silly adventures and went on an impromptu pub crawl, just like the good ole days. It was so cool going back to a city that I once lived in and, only a couple of years later, still knowing where everything was and having friends who were locals in town. My British accent came back almost immediately.

The next day, we took the Chunnel to Paris (the Channel Tunnel from the United Kingdom to France), and spent a couple of days with Radha's friends from her own study abroad adventure. We woke up one morning, both having a craving for chocolate. We looked at each other and blurted out at the same time: "Belgium!"

And off we went.

We jumped on the Eurail to Brussels in search of dark chocolate. As we were walking the narrow cobblestoned streets, we came across a handsome brown-haired boy about our age and an adorable, smiling blond girl also wearing large backpacks, and we got to talking with them.

They were Canadians and we were originally from Montreal, so we immediately connected. As it turned out, they were studying abroad in Amsterdam and were in Brussels for the weekend. They were having a hard time finding a place to stay in Brussels, so immediately, Radha and I offered up our hostel and told them that we could share our room with them. They were so grateful, and to return the favor, they invited us to stay at their student housing in Amsterdam. Perfect! We spent the night adventuring all over Brussels and finding a small club with a dance floor. We Canadians love to dance, so we broke it down together on the *Belgique* dance floor.

After our jaunt in Belgium, we accepted our new friends' offer and jumped the Eurail to Amsterdam. On the way to Amsterdam, we met a couple of Californian dudes who were traveling to Germany. They invited us to Berlin, and we caught up with them in Berlin once we left Amsterdam.

And that's just a sampling of how the entire adventure went. We met people along the way and bounced from Amsterdam, Berlin, Munich, Stuttgart, Zurich, and Interlaken to Milan, Florence, and then concluded our trip in Rome, and on the smallest student budget you could imagine.

Along the way, we had some of the most authentic local experiences possible, because we made it a point to go off the beaten path in each of the places we went. If we had been content mulling around London and Paris bars, I'm sure we would have had a great time but would not have had nearly as many unique experiences as we did.

One such experience was when Florence won the Coppa Italia, and we were directly southwest of downtown Florence at Le Murate, which was a former women's prison turned outdoor party space. The place was beautiful and you could tell from the high brick walls that this was once a marching grounds for prisoners.

When Florence won, the entire city went bananas, and all of a sudden, Le Murate turned into the biggest dance party in the entire city. We took part in the celebration and danced till sunrise. We found out about this place by befriending a random Italian dude at the statue of David and specifically asked him what the coolest thing to do in the city was. If we had simply made conversation and talked about the weather or where he was from, we might have missed out on one of my favorite experiences ever.

Another time, Rads and I passed a group of boys playing soccer on the street in Amsterdam and challenged them to a game. We ended up beating these boys in an all-out soccer showdown and had to go back the next day for a rematch because they refused to accept defeat. We ended up staying an extra night in Amsterdam to show them who was the boss. Yet again, another authentic, memorable experience.

The point here is that if your intent is to create memorable experiences wherever you go, put yourself in the best position to do that. What's the worst that could happen? They might say "I don't know where to have fun in town"? Those are odds I am always willing to take.

DO COOL SHIT TRAVEL TIPS

Always look for the most-fun people wherever you go. Search for the people laughing the most and those who seem most engaged with each other and their surroundings.

You could start by approaching a person or group and paying them a compliment—say that you like someone's shirt or tell them where you're from. Once you get to talking, ask them if they know where the cool local spots are that are off the beaten path or if they know of a unique party to go to. Having employed this tactic countless times, this question alone sometimes does the trick to get invited to a random house party that never in a million years would any other tourist have ever known about.

I even did this when I first moved to New York. I would walk up to random fun-looking people and tell them that I'm visiting from Montreal and wanted to experience something different. It really helped me to find the fun places to go in this massive city and not be limited to the reviews on Yelp or the events sections of the paper. After all, we all know that the most exciting people and parties won't exactly be found in an ad and are more likely to be discovered through a personal invite. If you give people the opportunity to be an expert, prepare to be delightfully surprised as they will most likely go out of their way to give you their best places to go.

The thing is, everyone wants to have exciting and authentic experiences, but few are willing to take real initiative. Taking the leap into the unknown has so many rewards! If you feel skittish, just take a deep breath and go up to the next group you see who looks interesting. See if one of them seems more approachable—and maybe there's a pause in the conversation that you watch for—and then go up to them, smile (smiles are the easiest and most effective things you could ever do!), and ask your question. The worst they can do is say they don't know, or roll their eyes. Listen—their loss for being so judgmental! Life will never reveal its inherent magic with that kind of attitude.

So here are some other ways to take initiative locally, when you travel for a quick getaway weekend or for an out-of-country adventure.

Local Adventure

A fast way to bring new adventure into your life is to be the person that creates new fun for your bored friends who do the same thing every weekend. Or go out by yourself. That's totally cool too! You will probably meet people along the way, and you'll see that your circle of friends will inevitably grow exponentially simply because there are so many others who want to do cool shit too.

Here are some fun things to do:

- **Geocaching:** It's a free treasure hunt anywhere in the world. People have stashed away these geocaches in every city and you can download the iPhone app and go on random adventures in search of these gems around town. Check it out at geocaching.com/iphone/. It makes for a unique experience and certainly a memorable one!
- **Live shows:** If you look in your city's local newspaper, you will likely find free shows, musicals, art exhibitions, or seminars all around the city. Don't even waste your time thinking if you'll like it or not—just go. For example, in New York, one of my favorite places to go is a great live music venue called Rockwood Music Hall. It's free to enter and the music is the best and most original in the city. I've met some great people at Rockwood because it's intimate and cozy and you can still have vibrant conversations with strangers (who often become friends) in between sets. The events you choose don't have to be musical live shows though. I've been going to the Moth—a storytelling series—for a while as well. It is

simply amazing and inspiring. You just have to seek these shows out. You'll be glad you did.

- *Sports:* Nothing beats the camaraderie that forms after a good game of dodgeball or kickball. There are leagues all over the major cities that pick up individual players who don't come with a full team and want to play. I formed several Urban Soccer teams in my day, and so many friendships were made this way.

The Authentic Travel Experience

In my opinion, in order to have the most authentic travel experience, this is what you need to do:

- **Create a Fun Fund:** Get a good group of friends (who you think really get along) and ask everyone to pool in $1,500 or $2,000 (or less, you can scale your trip to the income of the members of your group) per year that will go to the Fun Fund. Each year, two people will be appointed to manage the Fun Fund and will plan an epic trip somewhere awesome for one week.

    In this way, every single year you will have a surprise waiting for you with your favorite people. It will be something you look forward to forever because of the surprise element. We started doing this recently and it's incredibly exciting! Start saving now!

- **Rent your apartment on Airbnb.com:** Whenever I travel, I rent my apartment on Airbnb, which pretty much covers the entire cost of my trips. It's incredible. And not only does Airbnb give people the freedom and ability to travel almost anywhere for very little cost, it also gives you an opportunity to meet interesting people from all around the world. I love Airbnb. It's such a smart business.

- **Join the couch-surfing community:** There is no better way to connect with locals immediately wherever you go than through staying on their couch (Couchsurfing.com is a great resource). If you don't want to spend any money on lodging or simply want to experience the authentic way of life where you are, definitely join the interesting couch-surfing community. The one caveat is that in order to stay at other people's places for free, you must offer your place up as well for other couch surfers passing through town. My friends who use it swear by it and say that some of their closest international friendships were born from it.

- **Let festivals guide you:** Find the coolest festivals around the world and let them guide your experiences. You will be able to encounter local music, art, film, dance, and everything else authentic to the area if you revolve your travel around festivals. Some amazing festivals to check out at least once in a lifetime: Burning Man (of course), the Philadelphia Experience (PEX), Full Moon Party in Thailand, AfrikaBurn in South Africa, any Renaissance festival, Coachella, the Tribeca Film Festival. There are so many regional festivals all over the world—you simply need to research them. I am dying to find more obscure festivals so please post them on docoolshit.org!

- **Travel with no itinerary:** There is a real magic to getting lost. Allow yourself to lose your awareness of time. No need to chase train schedules, hotel bookings, flights, etc. Just go with the flow and you will find that your experiences will be that much more authentic if you simply travel with the intention of getting lost and losing your typical focus on time. Try it for just a few days; you can do it!

- **Fresh start:** Travel is a unique opportunity to get out of the hustle and bustle of everyday life and just *be*, wherever you are. Traveling by yourself from time to time is not a terrible thing to do. It encourages you to meet new people, get outside of yourself, and practice being the best version of yourself at all times. It also puts you in more unusual situations than if you had someone familiar with you amid your familiar surroundings and habits.

- **Ask yourself the important questions:** A great way to maximize impact on your trip is to go on vacation with intent and ask yourself a few questions along the way. Make sure you bring a journal to write down your thoughts, especially since we can learn so much about our patterns and the ways we get stuck from just looking back at what we've written. Here are some good questions to get your mind going:

- What am I neglecting in my life?
- What am I not doing that I want to be?
- What can I change in my life that can make me so much happier?
- What risk can I take right now that would add value to my life?

Things to Consider Every Time You Travel (Just in Case!)

- **Sleeping bag:** You just never know where you may end up.
- **Floor mat:** Again, you just never know where you may end up.
- **Pillow:** I literally cannot go anywhere without my pillow. Carry a good pillow, for goodness sake.

For the most part, when it comes to adventuring, just get outside your comfort zone and look for the authentic magic all around you. Go with intention and your life will be all the richer for it! I can't wait to hear your stories at docoolshit.org.

17

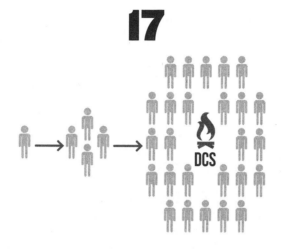

COMMUNITY IS EVERYTHING

How to Build Your Tribe

I am who I am because of who we all are.
—Ubuntu

Asif yelled into the loudspeaker, "On your mark . . . Get set . . . *Go!*" Rads and I took off as fast as we could. "Left, right, left, right, turn!!! Left, right, left, right . . ." As we hit the halfway point of the three-legged race (a race we, ahem, have won every year), we could see our top competition, Andrew and Dave, move past us.

We had already blown past Tony Hsieh and Dan Rollman (in addition to all six of the other teams competing in this final heat), and it was down to our two teams.

"Come on, let's go faster!" I yelled. We knew that our last shot at coming back and winning was if they messed up on the final turn.

As we approached the turn, Rads said, "Don't forget to start with your left foot after the turn!"

Out of the corner of our eyes, we saw Andrew and Dave get to their final turn.

Sure enough, their knees knocked into each other's, their third leg started to wobble, and that was our window of opportunity to go for gold.

We made the turn, left foot first, and shot past Andrew and Dave, who sprawled in the middle of the course. As we laughed and hugged, we couldn't help reveling in the fact that we remained Agra-Palooza's fifteenth-annual reigning champion of the three-legged race.

We looked around us—everyone was either laughing their faces off, rolling around in the grass with their partners attached to them, or trying to tenaciously run toward us to congratulate us with their legs still tied together. In that moment, all felt right in the world. Our community was together and happy.

Our childhood was all about games and functions. If it wasn't soccer games, it was badminton on Sundays and Hindi or Japanese functions on weekends.

For our birthdays, we threw two parties: one we called the kids birthday party and the other we called the adults birthday party. At the kids party, we invited all of our friends from school, and at the adult one, our parents invited all of their friends. It was basically an excuse to throw two birthday parties for us. But, hey, we didn't mind! That meant more presents for us! Since Yuri's birthday is January 28, and Radha's and mine is January 26, we threw most of our birthday parties together as kids.

Our parents made up two really fun games that all of our friends grew up with and looked forward to each year. One was called Lucky Dip, and the other was called Yes-No.

Lucky Dip was a game where our parents would put a bunch of candy and chocolate out on our sprawling basement floor and we would have to stand behind a line and throw an eight-inch ring around the goodies. Whatever candy the ring landed on, we got to keep. Of course my parents put the more expensive and decadent chocolates farther away, so it was harder to throw the ring around them.

Well, as you can imagine, kids who grew up playing this game from five years of age to eighteen years old would have enough experience at this point to take a running jump to launch themselves from the starting line in hopes to get the ring around the most expensive chocolate. It was amazing to see the progression and tenacity over the years.

The other game, Yes-No, was by far the most competitive at our birthday parties. My parents always started by warming up the group with questions like, "Miki is older than Radha—yes or no?" (Answer: No, of course not, can't you tell?) Then they would get right into it: "The current president of North Korea is ——, yes or no?" When you're six years old and playing this game, it's a bit terrifying.

There were two supernerds who kept winning Yes-No every year (Tejas and Vijay, you know who you are), and finally, after so many years, and much to everyone's surprise, at our eighteenth birthday party another kid in our class—Vikaas—won. To this day, I think Vikaas still has "Reigning Yes-No Champion" on his résumé and it is still a source of great pride (and a great conversation starter in interviews).

Having experienced this engaging ritual of games for all to enjoy and participate in for so many years, we loved how energized people were when they left the party and we wanted to continue these kinds of traditions. So when we moved out of the house, we started two more events, both still using the house and the surrounding pool and yard as our staging grounds: one that was called Agra-Palooza and the other our New Year's Eve Eve party that always happened on December 30, the day before New Year's Eve.

Agra-Palooza takes place the third week of July, when about fifty to seventy-five friends and family members descend on our parents' place for a sleepover weekend (basically every inch of the house is covered with people passed out). Picture the barbecue version of the Olympics except with chickpea curry and samosas on the snack table and veggie burgers on the grill. It has physical challenges like a three-legged race, egg toss, pool-diving competition, round-robin Ping-Pong tournament, volleyball, and basketball games. It culminates with martinis in the Jacuzzi and long conversations about world issues. People leave Agra-Palooza with deeper, more meaningful friendships and a feeling of togetherness.

New Year's Eve Eve is our "Intellectual Olympics," where my parents create riddles about the current events for the year and hide clues all over the house so guests have to run around, look for clues, solve the riddles, and then put the answers on a paper that had a hangman finish, where we would have to unscramble the final word. It is intense and always a blast.

One thing both parties have in common is the talent segment, where it's mandatory for all guests to come with a talent to share—either a song, dance, act, poem, scene, story, magic, yoga pose, art on the spot, or anything creative and expressive. It forces even the shyest of our friends to come out of their shells and perform in front of an audience.

There were other evenings of celebration and community as well. Whenever my parents had my dad's work friends over, they would do a night of poetry readings; his colleagues had to bring and perform a poem in front of everyone. Watching a bunch of engineers act out poetry was better than any comedy show imaginable.

On certain holidays, like Easter, we always wanted to come home not only because we wanted to hang out with our parents but also because they would create an intense, engineering-like Easter egg hunt where we had to solve geographic riddles to get to the eggs. "From base camp, walk eighty paces north-easterly and you will see a branch hanging ever so slightly over a babbling brook. Walk east from there, fifty paces, and you will find the egg nestled beneath a man-made creation." We loved the competition.

Every time a holiday came around, we knew we had something to look forward to, which of course encouraged us to go home for every holiday. Our parents figured us out!

I carried that method out with my friends once I moved out on my own, planning parties with games and activities. I mean, how many times can we go to parties where we just go, eat, hang out, talk, and leave? I've always believed that to get everyone to have a great time, and to feel a deepened connection within the group, there had to be participation from everyone, even the quieter ones. The goal was to have everyone leave feeling happier, more loved, more understood, and alive!

We didn't know it back then, but we were assembling the building blocks of a solid community: built with the foundation of unanimous participation.

This brings me to the event that defines unanimous participation: Burning Man.

As described in chapter 15, Burning Man is an art and music festival in the middle of the desert of Nevada, and it is, without a doubt, the utopian ideal of what "community" truly means.

This otherworldly festival started with just a few people in 1986 and has grown over the past twenty-seven years to an event that has a thriving community most likely in the hundreds of thousands and now draws sixty thousand people from around the world to participate. Each year.

Breathtakingly spectacular art installations are conceived and constructed, costumes are planned and fantastically created—even the cars are illuminated and designed with art in mind—and when you look around the desert and see the most creative and fantastical art, costumes, cars, and more, it's enough to bring even the most unsentimental to tears. For me, I'm moved because people are creating things for the love of it and the desire to share it with others, and not for any other reason.

This festival grew into what it has become partly because at the root of it all, humans naturally want to be able to express themselves in movement, style, art, poetry, or any which way they are inspired to do so; they want to be heard, understood, and to belong to something where they have an important role to play.

The founder, Larry Harvey, crafted a set of ten principles for Burning Man—basically, a set of guidelines for the ever-growing community.

He said that the principles "were crafted not as a dictate of how people should be and act, but as a reflection of the community's ethos and culture as it had organically developed since the event's inception."

Here are his ten principles. See if you're not just a little inspired by them. If you can imagine a world that lived by these principles, can you imagine what kind of world it would be?

RADICAL INCLUSION
Anyone may be a part of Burning Man. We welcome and respect the stranger. No prerequisites exist for participation in our community.

GIFTING
Burning Man is devoted to acts of gift giving. The value of a gift is unconditional. Gifting does not contemplate a return or an exchange for something of equal value.

DECOMMODIFICATION
In order to preserve the spirit of gifting, our community seeks to create social environments that are unmediated by commercial sponsorships, transactions, or advertising. We stand ready to protect our culture from such exploitation. We resist the substitution of consumption for participatory experience.

RADICAL SELF-RELIANCE
Burning Man encourages the individual to discover, exercise, and rely on his or her inner resources.

RADICAL SELF-EXPRESSION
Radical self-expression arises from the unique gifts of the individual. No one other than the individual or a collaborating group can determine its content. It is offered as a gift to others. In this spirit, the giver should respect the rights and liberties of the recipient.

Communal Effort

Our community values creative cooperation and collaboration. We strive to produce, promote, and protect social networks, public spaces, works of art, and methods of communication that support such interaction.

Civic Responsibility

We value civil society. Community members who organize events should assume responsibility for public welfare and endeavor to communicate civic responsibilities to participants. They must also assume responsibility for conducting events in accordance with local, state, and federal laws.

Leaving No Trace

Our community respects the environment. We are committed to leaving no physical trace of our activities wherever we gather. We clean up after ourselves and endeavor, whenever possible, to leave such places in a better state than when we found them.

Participation

Our community is committed to a radically participatory ethic. We believe that transformative change, whether in the individual or in society, can occur only through the medium of deeply personal participation. We achieve being through doing. Everyone is invited to work. Everyone is invited to play. We make the world real through actions that open the heart.

Immediacy

Immediate experience is, in many ways, the most important touchstone of value in our culture. We seek to overcome barriers that stand between us and a recognition of our inner selves, the reality of those around us, participation in society, and contact with a natural world exceeding human powers. No idea can substitute for this experience.

For me, the biggest thing that stood out for me in his ten principles was this one statement:

We achieve being through doing.

The notion that your most authentic self will come through simply by doing the things you love absolutely captivated me. It means that you will simply be exactly who you want to be when you start acting that way. For example, if you want to be fit, you have to act and go to the gym. If you want to be the best partner you can be, then act on the things that your partner asks of you (within reason of course) and give the kind of love that you'd like to receive in return. If you want to be financially successful, you have to work hard to get there.

I have built a solid tribe of stellar people in my life, and I am so grateful to be in a city like New York, where motivated people from all over the world are drawn by its magnetic energy.

From growing up in French Canadian, Japanese, and Indian communities to being part of competitive sports teams, Cornell, entrepreneurship groups, and the Burning Man community, I think I understand, for myself, in my own way, how to grow my own thriving community.

MY DO COOL SHIT GUIDE TO KEEPING AND GROWING A THRIVING TRIBE

The following ideas will help keep your tribe growing and thriving.

Express Happiness When You See Your People

There is no need to be too cool. When you see your friends and family, feel free to emphatically wag your tail when your friend walks in the door; it will always be well received. Show your excitement to see them. You will never regret showing too much love and they will love receiving it.

Let Everyone Share Stories and Participate

At the end of the day, everyone wants to be heard. Allow everyone to feel that way. We host storytelling nights because it brings our community together, makes the love and support get deeper and stronger, and it gives everyone a chance to tell stories.

NST: No Small Talk

Why do it? It's boring. Dig in. Find out what your family and friends are excited about. Or talk about love and relationships or some other juicy and personal topic. That's always fun and gets the conversation moving to a better place. Stop it with the "Did you have a good day today or a bad day today?" (Think a *Seinfeld* episode with Kramer.) Instead, ask "What was the most exciting thing that happened to you today?" Isn't that so much more fun to answer?

Give Credit as Often as You Can

In the same way people want to be heard, people want to be recognized. Recognize your peers when they do cool shit. They will want to keep doing it.

Give Confidence—It's Free

I love genuinely complimenting my people and making them feel confident. It's free; it makes them feel good, more comfortable, and safe. As soon as people feel confident, their authentic selves shine through and that's when real, genuine bonding happens. As soon as you're just you without any front or pretense, it will give permission for everyone around you to be exactly who they are. This will help foster an environment for everyone to just be himself or herself.

Challenge Your People to Push Themselves

Compliments are great, but also make sure that your people are doing the best they can to be their best selves. If you think you can help, say something and help them—but do it nicely and patiently.

Be as Honest as You Can

People will just respect you more for it, and only with honesty can you really break through to people's hearts and minds.

Take Three Long, Deep Breaths When Faced with Challenging Circumstances

Hey, we're all passionate people, and sometimes it can get to us negatively. When faced with a tough situation with a friend or family member, do your best to take three long, deep breaths and do everything in your power not to lose your cool. Taking these breaths usually will do the trick, and it can help move through any tension or reaction you may have been feeling. It will also maintain harmony in your circle.

Be as Creative as You Can with Your Friends

Be the initiator. Come up with fun things for people to do. The more you do it, the more fun you will have and it may even inspire others to want to create unique experiences for you as well.

Adopt a "Help First" Mentality

You will get more from your community if you seek to help others before trying to get others to help you. Simply ask this question to the people you care about: "Is there anything I can do to help?" It is one of the easiest ways to show someone you truly care for them and it will usually make people want to reciprocate. But don't expect reciprocation. Just engage in service and watch out, because the universe likes to serve back what you give.

Connect People!

Always be thinking about who you know who could help your community. Make connections where both parties stand to benefit and you will be associated with any good that comes from the relationship in perpetuity. Don't expect to get anything from it. Just know that you are spreading goodwill for your tribe, and again, the universe is always watching.

What core values can you create for your circle of friends? Let them be known. Organize a fun night with your friends and come up with a few that make the most sense to you and your group. Then do your best to live by them!

Before you start thinking about creating a community, remember these two things:

1. **Don't make friends just to make friends. Build the *right* community who will give you the strength to act on your ideas and inspire you to be the best version of you.**
2. **Building and growing a community is so much more about what you put in than what you get out.**

A perfect example of this is my good friend Elliott Bisnow. He started Summit Series, an incredible entrepreneurship community, because he wanted to make like-minded friends and meet new, interesting people who he admired and wanted to share ideas with.

He started out by calling up a group of up-and-coming entrepreneurs who he wanted to meet and invited them on a ski trip. He spent time and money organizing an incredible event for interesting movers and shakers, where they skied, shared business ideas, had great bonding dinners, and partied together.

Once the trip was over, he had a group of twenty smart, talented ambassadors to go and spread the message of growing this community. The following year, there were a hundred people who attended, then it grew to seven hundred people, and now it's more than one thousand people strong, including among them the likes of Sir Richard Branson and Tony Hsieh.

Elliott built this community because he put in the effort to make the calls, invite entrepreneurs out, and execute a wonderful, memorable event, time and time again. He understood the meaning of the phrase, "You get out of an experience what you put in."

Another smaller example is our pizza-making class at my restaurant. In addition to it being an additional revenue stream for us, we get to teach a new craft to our participating guests and have their undivided attention for three hours, which means that when they leave, they become brand ambassadors for the restaurant. They get to know us, what we do, why we work with local farms, experience the yummy food, etc., and they are able to spread the message more knowledgeably than before. We're putting in the time and effort to teach people a new skill, and in return we get to build our tribe of ambassadors! It's MB, through and through.

So, you see, doing cool shit is really all about what you put in! People feel so much more fulfilled and take more pride in the community knowing they had a contributing role to play, rather than participating as just a spectator.

Now your challenge is to go out and find those like-minded people and create a fun event that will bring them to you! You will start building your tribe in no time and having an incredible life story as a result!

I am excited for you to seek out your community, and I look forward to your stories at docoolshit.org.

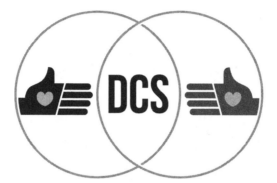

GIVING BACK

Why Service Matters

The best way to find yourself is to lose yourself in the service of others.
—Gandhi

Inner-City High School Classroom, the Bronx, New York

Reaching down for the door handle while holding a stack of pizza boxes wasn't exactly the most graceful thing, but I managed to twist the knob and push the door open with my hip.

As I entered the Bronx high school classroom, I felt a flurry of quizzical eyes turn my way, and with one nod toward the teacher, I looked back at the sea of questioning fourteen-year-olds as I tried to straighten the pizza boxes in hand.

"Who wants pizza?"

That seemed to be the secret password, as the whole classroom went bananas! Next thing I knew, I was surrounded by happy faces and greedy hands as the kids couldn't wait to have a bite of their favorite food.

Immediately, I was *in*. As you know by now, free food does it every time.

I watched them inhale the pizzas, smack their lips, and look to see if there were seconds. They loved it!

I waited for the classroom to settle down to get their full attention.

I then said, "Do you know what you just ate?"

In unison, they yelled, "Pizza!"

"What did it taste like?"

"Pizza!"

"Did you like it?"

"Love it!!" they shrieked.

"OK, well, did you know that the crust was made of whole-wheat flour?"

All of a sudden, their reactions shifted.

"Ewww!" they yelled.

"Did you know that we slow cook our marinara sauce and naturally sweeten the sauce with fresh onions from a local farm?"

"Ewwww! Onions are gross!" they all said.

"Well, you can't say that now that you already told me that you loved it, can you?"

All of a sudden those very same eyes that had started to glimmer with suspicion and disapproval started to show a deeper understanding. I smiled. It was as though I could actually see a lightbulb go off inside them.

Almost instantly, whole-wheat crust and fresh vegetables in a sauce got approval because they were tasty and it gave the students a much easier entry point into being open to the idea of healthy foods. It was the perfect icebreaker for talking about the difficult and sometimes complicated topic of nutrition.

It opened a great two-way conversation and discussion about food, food stigmas, and food issues that these inner-city kids were facing.

We talked about their passions and what they wanted to be when they grow up and how they were going to get there. This conversation really helped them understand that besides hard work, dedication, and passion, eating healthy was going to help them become everything they ever wanted to be because they needed to properly fuel their bodies in order to have the energy required to be focused and work hard. The kids were jazzed by this honest conversation.

I walked out of the classrooms feeling more energized and fulfilled than ever. I felt like I might have played a small part in making a positive change in these adolescents' lives and it made me feel so good to know that a seed was planted for a better, healthier life.

I wanted to chase that good feeling over and over again. And I did! I've been to more than fifty classrooms and even got invited to address the United Nations Global Youth Summit to talk about nutrition, social entrepreneurship, hopes, and dreams, and I want to continue to do more!

Giving back and volunteering is one of those things that most of us rarely think about unless there is a disaster in our backyard—like 9/11 or Hurricane Sandy. In those instances, the entire city of New York came together and became a community of people helping people. They didn't ask for anything back; they simply gave to others and the city was closer than ever.

Why can't that warm feeling toward our communities happen without the disaster part attached to it? Why can't we help each other out with no strings attached? Like real, old-school neighbors who would bring a casserole to the new neighbors or help to shovel their neighbors' driveways if they are elderly or sick? (That's a shout-out to you, Mark D.—you were a great neighbor to my parents.) Why can't it just be that way all the time?

Once you have those feelings of elation, you'll want to continue to seek that feeling and keep doing the things that bring you back to that experience. It's fulfilling to the heart, and it makes a lasting impression on not only your life but also the lives of others. People remember the times they gave back to their communities far more than the time they bought those expensive shoes.

I should also quickly mention that there are some great ancillary benefits that stem from volunteering. Some of the ones you might discover yourself are that:

- You will meet other like-minded, caring humans and start new friendships.
- Maybe you'll find love when you volunteer.
- You can deepen your existing relationships. For example, ask a coworker or new friend to go with you to volunteer and you will see how much stronger your friendship or relationship will become.

Do Cool Shit Task

Volunteer somewhere. Don't delay! Identify an issue you care about and seek it out. There are often multiple ways to volunteer, such as by serving meals at a local mission or church, providing tutoring or mentorship to a young girl or boy, or by helping the elderly in your neighborhood. Once you have the chance to serve, see how you feel once you're done.

I bet that once you start, you will want to increase the frequency, so all I am asking you to do is just volunteer once! Go and help a cause that means something to you and it may very well create an awesome pattern for yourself and others! And once you do, I want to hear all about it, so please post your experience on docoolshit.org.

19

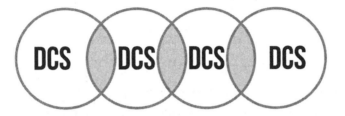

YOU ARE AS COOL AS THE FRIENDS YOU KEEP

What Cool Shit My Friends Are Up To

Questions are eternal. The answers are temporary.

—Dr. Deb

One of my favorite sayings goes, "I am who I am because of who we all are." I am really happy with the people I spend most of my time with. I am inspired, motivated, and rejuvenated by them; most of all, I am excited to learn from them.

I asked these people the same five questions to see how similar or different their answers would be. I got an interesting array of responses, which I will share with you now.

1. **What does "doing cool shit" mean to you?**
2. **What cool shit are you up to? And what cool shit are you planning in the future?**
3. **What was the most important lesson you've learned about doing cool shit in business?**

4. **What is the best life advice you can give to help someone else do
   cool shit?**

5. **What was the moment in your life that made you realize that you
   could stray from the norm and do cool shit?**

TIM FERRISS—AUTHOR OF *THE 4-HOUR WORKWEEK* **AND** *THE 4-HOUR BODY*

I met Tim at Summit at Sea. We bonded while canoeing in the Bahamas
together. He's the author of *The 4-Hour Workweek*, which is an international bestseller and incredibly entertaining book about how to kick ass
efficiently in business and how to also do cool shit in life, like win at the
World Tango Dancing Championship. He is a master with words, and I
am fascinated by the way he thinks. See for yourself.

1. What does "doing cool shit" mean to you?

To me, "doing cool shit" has two parts. Part one: focusing my time—the
most valuable nonrenewable resource—on things that get me really excited. As Derek Sivers would say: The response has to be "No" or "Hell
yes!" and nothing in between.

Part two: teaching others to do the same in a scalable way. This leads
to some really uncommon and awesome outcomes, whether for-profit,
nonprofit, or not-thinking-of-profit. My general guiding tenet is from
Mark Twain: "Whenever you find yourself on the side of the majority,
it's time to pause and reflect."

2. What cool shit are you up to? And what cool shit are you planning
in the future?

Trying to scale education reform by advising start-ups like Donors
Choose.org. Disrupting big industries and creating new industries by
advising other for-profit start-ups like Uber, Evernote, and perhaps fifteen others. These founders all keep me on my toes. Entrepreneurship
is a full-contact sport.

**3. What was the most important lesson you've learned about doing
cool shit in business?**

There's no one path to success, but there is one sure path to failure:
trying to make everyone happy. I learned that from Bill Cosby, actually.
He is incredible. Watch the documentary *Comedian* for examples.

4. What is the best life advice you can give to help someone else do cool shit?

Besides what I've already mentioned: you are the average of the five
people you associate with most.

**5. What was the moment in your life that made you realize that you could
stray from the norm and do cool shit on your own?**

Probably when I held my first accelerated learning seminar during college. I'd been making $6 to $8 an hour working in the attic of a library all
semester beforehand. Then I sold out the three-hour seminar—thirty or
so seats at $50 a pop—for a total of $1,500. I remember getting on my bike
afterward, feeling as if I were floating on air. It was like a dream, a hal-
lucination. I had loose change and handwritten checks stuffed in all my
pockets and bunched up in my fists, even as I rode. I've never felt richer.

In retrospect, it wasn't just the money. I was creating something
from nothing that got me high. And that's a drug I'm willing to sell.

ELLIOTT BISNOW—FOUNDER OF SUMMIT SERIES

I met Elliott on the boat at his conference. My experience at Summit
at Sea brought me more fantastic relationships with like-minded people
than ever before. I cannot be more grateful to Elliott for creating a
fun environment for excited entrepreneurs looking forward to making a
positive impact in the world.

1. What does "doing cool shit" mean to you?

It means thinking big. In fact, thinking bigger than you ever thought
possible. Building businesses or organizations that can truly affect the

world and change neighborhoods, cities, or even entire industries. We are in the midst of an entrepreneurial revolution and opportunities are everywhere to affect those around you. Think big.

2. What cool shit are you up to? And what cool shit are you planning in the future?
Summit, the company which I started, is purchasing Powder Mountain, the largest ski resort by acreage in North America. We think that we can not only preserve the heritage and culture of this iconic and beloved ski resort but also that on the backside of the mountain, we can build a community for entrepreneurs and thinkers who are making a positive impact on the world.

3. What was the most important lesson you've learned about doing cool shit in business?
Waking up early, putting in fifteen hours a day and leaving your heart and soul on the table only works if you love what you're doing. Doing incredible and cool work allows you to put all your effort and energy into the project because you truly are in love with what you're doing and the impact you're having.

4. What is the best life advice you can give to help someone else do cool shit?
Think big. At Summit, we always ask ourselves how we can think bigger. Keep pushing. Keep believing. Take what you're working on and push it to the next level. Believe in your vision and go for it.

5. What was the moment in your life that made you realize that you could stray from the norm and do cool shit on your own?
Freshman year of college I met the resident adviser for my dorms. He lived on the floor below me. One day I saw him screen printing T-shirts, and he explained to me how he had his own business. I was blown away someone could start their own company. I'd never actually seen someone have one at my age. From there, I dreamed of being an entrepreneur every day.

MARIE FORLEO—FOUNDER OF MARIEFORLEO.COM AND RHH B-SCHOOL

I met Marie at a Crunch Gym in the West Village when I was doing a pizza tasting for gym members. She came up to my table and asked me immediately if I was the owner. I said, "Why yes, I am," and she said, "I knew it! You act like it." And then we chatted for a little while and exchanged numbers. She sent me a text a few minutes later saying, "This may sound really weird, but I think we were meant to be friends." I remember smiling reading that. The very next day, my friend Heather invited me to a small intimate birthday dinner with eight people and I sat down and introduced myself to everyone. I looked to my right and couldn't believe who it was: Marie. We both looked at each other and burst out laughing. And then we hugged. And we've been friends ever since. Out of the entire city, of all the birthday parties and dinners going on, we both found ourselves at the same one, the day after we met. Marie has a successful company called Rich Happy and Hot and has her own online business school for women who want to start their own businesses.

1. What does "doing cool shit" mean to you?
Living and creating exactly how you want to. It's about choosing to spend your time and resources on projects that light you up and being unapologetic about saying no to everything else.

2. What cool shit are you up to? And what cool shit are you planning in the future?
Creating the world's most enjoyable and effective school for modern entrepreneurs at JoinBschool.com, using a portion of profits to build schools with Pencils of Promise, and continuing to grow and expand our weekly inspirational and educational show at MarieTV.com—we now have viewers in virtually every country in the world.

3. What was the most important lesson you've learned about doing cool shit in business?

Mastering how to market your products and services with heart, soul, and transparency is the most valuable skill you can have if you want to succeed in business and make a positive impact on the world.

4. What is the best life advice you can give to help someone else do cool shit?

Everything is figure-out-able. No longer can you let the excuse of not knowing how to do something stop you. Just go online and Google that shit up! Thanks to the Internet, mobiles, and social media, we now have the world (and each other) at our fingertips. No matter what you want to learn, explore, or create, you have power to figure it out and make it happen.

5. What was the moment in your life that made you realize that you could stray from the norm and do cool shit on your own?

It was the early 2000s in NYC. At about 2:30 a.m., I came home from bartending, opened my e-mail, and saw that I sold my first e-book online. That moment made me realize I could use my imagination, my passion, and the power of technology to change lives around the world and earn a great living while I did something I truly believed in.

SOPHIA BUSH—ACTRESS AND SPOKESPERSON

I met Sophia on a small boat on my way to a tiny island off the coast of Panama over New Year's 2013. Thirty friends and friends of friends adventured together for an unforgettable trip to San Blas Islands for four days of fun in the sun.

I'll always remember her dimples when she smiled and introduced herself to me. I didn't recognize her because I never grew up watching much television, but I found out that she was a lead in the show *One Tree Hill*, an American series that ran for nine seasons. She is still acting and is a spokesperson for several charities.

1. What does "doing cool shit" mean to you?

Cool shit, to me, is positive disruption. It shakes things up. That can be on a personal level, a community level, or even a global level. What are you doing, or making, that's making the world around you a better place? You can be making dinner for friends or inventing something. All of this pushes us in a direction of positivity.

2. What cool shit are you up to? And what cool shit are you planning in the future?

For the first time in a decade I've paused. I am pursuing my passions, not just my career. I've taken the last few months to really answer a valuable question for myself: "What do you *want* to do today?" I've begun writing again. I am traveling for my favorite philanthropies and organizations. I just opened two schools that I built with Pencils of Promise in Guatemala. I am advising and investing in tech companies, and I am chasing the sun around the globe. Very cool shit. My plan from here on out is to deepen my effectiveness as an activist, an adviser, and a creator in all walks of my life.

3. What was the most important lesson you've learned about doing cool shit in business?

You have to do the thing, or things, that keep you up at night. Working toward a paycheck is what the world teaches us to do. But if you work on your *life*, on the things that light a fire in you, the money will come while you are creating real change or goodness; while you are making things that matter. I have started asking myself two questions: "What makes you angry?" As in, what makes you want to storm the castle in this world? And "What makes you so excited that you can talk about it for hours?" The answers to those questions are the things I'm choosing to pursue.

4. What is the best life advice you can give to help someone else do cool shit?

First, take a moment and make sure that you are coming from a starting place of kindness. Then speak your truth! It will be scary.

But run toward it. Try to do so fearlessly, or despite your fear. Because your truth, the thing that lights a fire inside of you, is a huge part of who you are. If you dull it, or dim it down, to try to make others comfortable, you will just make yourself small and lessen your chances of being effective. The best way to elevate others is to elevate yourself. So be big. Be bold. Speak it, shout it, from rooftops and the peaks of mountains. Love your fire. Breathe it into other people. And you will inspire them to do the same. Then we all get bigger and better.

5. What was the moment in your life that made you realize that you could stray from the norm and do cool shit on your own?
When I started to realize that my voice mattered. I started to use social media to have conversations about causes that inspire me, music that gets me dancing, style that knocks my socks off, and the responses I started getting blew me away! I realized that my authenticity—my nerd-fests and freak-outs and passionate diatribes—mattered to the people that matter to me. And that changed the game for good.

GRAHAM HILL—FOUNDER OF *TREEHUGGER* AND LIFEEDITED
I met Graham Hill when I was twenty-three years old. I would like to say that Graham was the person who introduced me to the world of entrepreneurship and made it seem possible. I met him standing in line to get into a party in 2003. Graham founded an awesome blog called TreeHugger.com and he sold it to Discovery Channel a few years later. He started another design concept called LifeEdited, which brings smart design to small spaces.

We had a blast that night at the party, and he invited me to brunch the next day in Chinatown at a place called DimSum Go Go. (I'll never forget it because it was at this brunch that I met Anne Maffei and Upendra Shardanand. Both Anne and Upes were go-getter entrepreneurs, and they really took me under their wings and invited me to so many different events and parties over the next few years and introduced me to other people doing awesome stuff. It was with their guidance, inspiration, and blessings that I was able to open my first business. Thank you guys so much!)

1. What does "doing cool shit" mean to you?

From a business perspective, it would mean acting as a catalyst to bring beautiful, useful, world-changing things into the world. Creating things that matter and that resonate with people . . .

2. What cool shit are you up to now? And what cool shit are you planning in the future?

I'm building a movement around less stuff and less space. I believe that we can apply design, technology, and behavior change to create fulfilling, compelling lives that allow us to live within our means financially and environmentally, and that simplifying our lives will give us a little more time, a little more ease, and perhaps a little more happiness. My company, LifeEdited, is focused on working with developers to build large buildings composed of small spaces paired with sharing systems and heavy on community. We are also looking to create small-space enabling housewares and furniture.

3. What was the most important lesson you've learned about doing cool shit in business?

At the end of the day, it's all about the product. Sure, you can help things along with marketing blah blah blah but it's pretty much about the product. Make some good shit!

4. What is the best life advice you can give to help someone else do cool shit?

Find some shit you love. Focus in that area. And notice that entrepreneurs aren't that special, they just figure it out and keep moving the ball forward.

5. What was the moment in your life that made you realize that you could stray from the norm and do cool shit on your own?

Don't think I had that moment . . . just realized at some point that that was what I was doing.

ADAM RICH—FOUNDER OF *THRILLIST*

Adam Rich is part of the Summit community as well. The world just keeps getting smaller and smaller. I brought some pizzas over to his office, and he gave me a tour of his impressive, growing workplace, and as we walked the floors, I could really see a sense of great pride in what he has accomplished thus far.

1. What does "doing cool shit" mean to you?

On the most basic level "doing cool shit" means putting energy in. It's the opposite of coasting along and following a groove. No matter what the "shit" in question is, if it's going to be "cool," it's got to feel exciting and fresh. Doing something others haven't requires an investment in thought, bravery, and effort and represents a basic way you interface with the world at large: Do you accept what you see around you and accept it as immutable, or do you perceive it as a starting point? Honestly, I don't think the scale of the endeavor is really that important. It's a binary characteristic: either you put energy in, or you don't.

2. What cool shit are you up to now? And what cool shit are you planning in the future?

Right now we are rethinking what we do at *Thrillist*. After putting out a men's lifestyle e-mail for the last seven-plus years, we're right now going through a really exciting period of unsentimentally reassessing everything we do. Seven years is an eternity in media, so as nerve-racking as it's been to call into question everything we know about our company, it's actually brought me closer back to the excitement I felt starting the company in the first place. I've realized that over these seven years, the evolving and refining we've done had turned our start-up into the exact kind of legitimate machine that inspires entrepreneurs to ask what they can do to push things further. I'm just excited that—in this instance—that entrepreneur can be me.

3. What was the most important lesson you've learned about doing cool shit in business?

To be transparent and treat people with respect.

4. What is the best life advice you can give to help someone else do cool shit?

Go for it. After conferences and panels, I talk to so many would-be entrepreneurs who don't have a website or anything concrete to show for their ambitions. My personal experience is that no matter how long you agonize over getting your initial offering perfectly right, once it's out there, you're showing it around, using it in the real world, you're going to find flaws and need to revise. Knowing that you can't ace it right off the bat, it's really just a question of grabbing your balls and jumping in with the best you can do. You either have a business or you don't, and not having a business is a surefire way to not have a successful business.

5. What was the moment in your life that made you realize that you could stray from the norm and do cool shit on your own?

I honestly don't think there was ever a point when the music swelled and I realized "I can do this!" Starting *Thrillist* was extremely stressful and scary, and it was only through years of working hard for incremental successes that I felt confident that it would all pan out. No matter how great you think your idea is, if you're not in there every day with your sleeves rolled up, it really doesn't matter.

I will say that—right before launch—I harassed and pestered every single person I knew and badgered them to sign up for our newsletter. Most were people I thought it would serve: young mostly guys living in NYC eager to feel like they were spending their time and money wisely in a city where you never have enough of either. My pitch was a personal one, since I created *Thrillist* because I felt the same way. What we sought—and still seek—to do is cut through the clutter, and with a trusted voice offer our readers a clear-eyed recommendation of some new thing they should check out. The tagline was "Here's the move." We sent our very first newsletter out to six hundred people.

CAPT. ZACHARY ISCOL—FOUNDER OF HIREPURPOSE

I met Zach in college at Uris Library. I remember we were both student athletes and were cramming for a test. We dated during our sophomore year and transitioned to best friends ever since. His family is like my second family and has been instrumental in so many of my life decisions.

When we graduated, Zach became a captain in the Marine Corps and served during the Iraq War. He earned a bronze star, and he had far too many close calls, but was somehow spared. He produced a documentary film called *The Western Front* with my sister Rads about the war in the Middle East and has since founded the company Hirepurpose to help veterans get jobs when they leave active duty, since he found that the government and military didn't properly help the veterans transition to civilian lives.

1. What does "doing cool shit" mean to you?

To me, doing cool shit means challenging the system and figuring out a better way of doing something. You can't be afraid of criticism, ridicule, or failure. Think about Magellan setting out to circumnavigate the world. Most people probably thought he was nuts because he was challenging popularly accepted truths. It is easy to look back and think, "Wow, all those people back then were crazy. How silly to think the world could be flat." But how often do we do the same thing today when faced with new technologies or ways of doing business? But those crazy ideas change the world. It isn't about making money or becoming successful, it is about challenging the status quo and striking out on your own in order to create something, do something that's never been done before, make meaningful change, and leave your mark.

2. What cool shit are you up to? And what cool shit are you planning in the future?

I served in the Marines and did a number of combat deployments overseas. In my last job in the service, I had the opportunity to help build and run the recruiting, screening, assessment, and selection program for US Marine Corps Special Operations. Essentially, that's how we find and select the right marines for special operations. After I got out, I started helping a few of my former marines find jobs and quickly realized that the entire online employment industry was built on a preindustrial technology—the résumé. Even the most technologically advanced job sites use powerful software applications to attempt to match key words in résumés with key words in a job description. For veterans, this is especially challenging because their military skills do not translate well to civilian jobs. So over the course of eight months, we took part of the methodology we used to screen and select marines for Special Operations and used it to build a sophisticated online platform (hirepurpose.com) to match top veterans with great jobs and internships. Unlike other military job sites, we dig deeper than just the résumé and introduce veterans to companies through employment testing that measures soft skills and behavioral strengths and personal profiles that enable veterans to better tell their stories to potential employers. Eventually, I'd like to use this to help everyone, not just military veterans, find meaningful employment that suits their interests, motivations, and strengths.

3. What was the most important lesson you've learned about doing cool shit in business?

Don't be afraid of failure. There is no such thing. You can only fail if you fail to learn from setbacks. If you're open and honest to it, failing is the best teacher and the only way to challenge assumptions that stand in the way of better products and, ultimately, success. But you also have to be willing to really lay it all out there and work your ass off. Otherwise you're just going to fail because you're lazy.

4. What is the best life advice you can give to help someone else do cool shit?
Don't be afraid to try new things. To be alive today and live in the developed world means you have more freedom of choice than at any point in history. Even one generation ago, your chosen profession remained your career for life. Take advantage of the fact that that's no longer the case. If you're not happy, try something else on for size until you are. Time is the most precious commodity.

5. What was the moment in your life that made you realize that you could stray from the norm and do cool shit on your own?
I was never the fastest kid, and I was never the smartest kid. That meant I didn't have much choice. If I was going to be successful, I was going to have to invent my own game.

DAN ROLLMAN—FOUNDER OF RECORDSETTER
I met Dan Rollman at my friend Nazli's party. He was by far the tallest guy in the room at six feet seven inches. I met him while he was helping my sister build a dresser in our new apartment. It took them seven hours to build the dresser. Dan founded RecordSetter after he was inspired by the Burning Man camp Playa Book of Records, where the camp would give out badges to anyone who set a random record about anything. With that whimsical idea, he thought to himself, "Why not create the Wikipedia of World Records?" and the idea grew from there. I love it and I am proud to say that I hold three world records on RecordSetter .com.

1. What does "doing cool shit" mean to you?
"Cool shit" happens when you find the courage to follow your gut and then execute to the best of your abilities.

**2. What cool shit are you up to? And what cool shit are you
planning in the future?**

Right now, I'm focused primarily on RecordSetter, a Burning Man–inspired media company that invites anyone, anywhere to set any world record they want. I also work on the National Day of Unplugging, a project designed to get people offline for one day a year. In my spare time, I make handwritten T-shirts (snerko.com).

The future is TBD, but possible "cool shit" projects include an Internet-free coffee shop, a line of Russian doll envelopes, a sport that combines miniature golf and bowling, and the World's Largest Menorah.

**3. What was the most important lesson you've learned about doing
cool shit in business?**

The only thing stopping you from doing cool shit is yourself. Don't rely on outside events or other people to make things happen. Put your head down, focus on your vision, and work, work, work.

4. What is the best life advice you can give to help someone else do cool shit?

Two answers:

- Solicit outside opinions, but ultimately learn to trust your gut.
- Don't try to do too much cool shit at once. Write down your ten best ideas. Cross out nine of them. Give all your love and energy to your biggest idea—the one that keeps you up at night. If you can successfully focus on a singular vision, good things will happen.

**5. What was the moment in your life that made you realize that you could
stray from the norm and do cool shit on your own?**

I used to work in advertising. Over the years, I watched several coworkers quit lucrative positions so they could follow their creative passions. One became a director, two wrote books, one produced a TV series, and another started a greeting card company. Watching these friends give up money and comfort in return for a deeper sense of satisfaction was tremendously inspiring. They gave me the courage to follow in their footsteps and take a similar path of my own.

RADHA AGRAWAL—MY TWIN SISTER

1. What does "doing cool shit" mean to you?

It means using the arts to shift culture. It means creating and following unique experiences that push one's physical and mental limits. Most important, it's service through community and laughter. Doing cool shit has to feel good, right?

2. What cool shit are you up to? And what cool shit are you planning in the future?

I started my company, Super Sprowtz, to shift the culture around nutrition and wellness education through the arts and media for preschool and elementary school children. There seemed to be a disconnect in the storytelling vis-à-vis nutrition education, and no one had created a solution that spoke to children first (i.e., that made it fun!), and so it seemed like the best place to start to really effect change from the ground up. Our goal is to be the default destination, whether through our educational products or online, for all things nutrition and ultimately environment education for parents. Our company mantra is "It has to be as entertaining as it is educational." We have many, many exciting plans for Super Sprowtz, so stay tuned!

3. What was the most important lesson you've learned about doing cool shit in business?

If you don't have a product you believe in and is worth waking up for in the morning and feeling a sense of purpose toward, you're not doing cool shit. I believe in our double bottom line of doing good and doing well. Otherwise, it feels pointless. Also: go big or go home. You have to want it so badly because, man, entrepreneurship is hard work! Also, pick a passionate team who will take the trash out with you at night.

4. What is the best life advice you can give to help someone else do cool shit?

- Hang your hat on something you believe in.
- In the end, there are no rules.
- Learn balance. Work hard and play hard. You gain a lot of perspective from playing hard after you've worked a long day.
- Give, give, give.
- Nothing is perfect. Just get going and get started and learn to iterate. Once the energy is out there, it will live.

5. What was the moment in your life that made you realize that you could stray from the norm and do cool shit on your own?

I've had so many moments that affirmed why this was the right path for me, but I think my "AHA!" moment was when I was designing a children's menu for *WILD*. I would sit with the kids who came in and color and tell stories about the superhero vegetable characters. I would watch child after child run to the counter and order more vegetables for his or her pizza. They would say, "Mom! I want more broccoli because I want to be super strong like Brian Broccoli!" I knew then I was on to something exciting and culture shifting, and the idea grew from there. My first leadership example was when I guided Miki out of the womb. I came out first and led the way five minutes before you entered the world.

DOING COOL SHIT

An Exercise in Evolution

So as you can see from reading my story, I am not the same person I was eight years ago, when I launched my first business at twenty-six years old. I learned so much about myself through creating a business and putting it out into the world. And every step of this journey has changed my outlook on life.

WHAT I LEARNED

I don't get scared anymore when I encounter something unfamiliar. I remember the first time I received tax documents from the IRS for my business, I freaked out. They were complicated (I swear it takes the IRS five pages to say what a normal human being would say in one), and the way the IRS communicates is just so cold and awful and their rules and demands were unfamiliar territory. Now, since I've seen these documents come in the mail many more times, it's not scary anymore. I simply send the docs to my accountant and he takes care of it (thanks,

Raj). It's old hat, and I know now that everyone gets the same documents and it's just standard procedure when you run a business.

I also learned that there is no point ever in freaking out. It solves zero problems! Nobody really knows exactly what they are doing in business when they first start, even if they've been to business school, but over time, we see patterns, experience familiar ups and downs, and the way we deal with issues gets easier and easier.

I remember the time I first had to let a manager go. I avoided the confrontation for as long as I could, but I knew that keeping this person in this management position was screwing things up for the business in the long run. I was scared to have the conversation and start over by myself again, but it was this experience that taught me how to face challenging circumstances. Now, if I ever feel scared or uncomfortable about something or someone, I can face it and know that I will always come out stronger and with more understanding because of it.

I learned that making good business relationships is no different than making good friends. Trust needs to be built, honoring your word is important, and having a good time getting to know the other is equally important.

One of the most important things in business and in life is that we have to be OK letting things go. It may be hard but it's the key to positive change. Releasing things actually feels so good and it can even *save* your life!

For instance, do you know how to catch a raccoon? No? OK, I'll tell you.

The best way to catch a raccoon is to create a small hole in the mud. Put spikes on the sides facing inward, and put a nut down in the bottom of the hole. The raccoon will put his paw in the hole and grab the nut. If he tries to pull his paw out while holding the nut, the spikes will rip his arm out and he will die. However, if he lets go of the nut, his arm will safely come out of the hole. The tragedy is that the raccoon will never let go of the nut and eventually he will die. The moral of the story is: let the nut go! The things that you are holding so dear will mean nothing if you will die trying to hold on to them.

> ## Do Cool Shit Exercise
>
> Detach yourself from your business. Take a 1,000-meter approach and look at where your business was when it started, where it is now, and where it can go. See what things could be improved if you could lose your attachment to them and be open to change. Is there anything holding back your business or anything that no longer fits? Holding on to things for the sake of nostalgia doesn't make sense. Life and work is iterative. Doing cool shit is an exercise in evolution.

MY NEXT ITERATIVE PROJECT

Most recently (and completely separate from pizza), I launched my new company THINX (www.shethinx.com) with my business partners Antonia Dunbar and Rads (of course). We found our inspiration for THINX through a problem that all women have. As busy women, we'd sometimes forget when our "time of the month" would arrive, and we'd have accidents and embarrassing situations (and ruined clothes). We realized that pretty much all of our girlfriends have had the same experience. We couldn't believe that there had been no innovation in undergarments for women that properly dealt with this issue. Over the course of three years, and after what seemed like a million iterations, we developed a patented line of underwear that is leak- and stain-resistant, breathable, and beautiful! We realized that there was no pair of underwear in the marketplace that thought of girls and women and protected us every day of the month.

We also realized that there was a massive problem in developing countries where women currently use sticks, old rags, and leaves to manage their monthly issue, and more than 67 million women in Africa alone have missed a week of school and dropped out early. So, we partnered up with AFRIpads, a Ugandan-based organization that creates washable, reusable cloth pads so that girls could easily afford them and go back to school and work without worrying. For every pair of underwear we sell, we fund the production of seven washable pads.

Buy one = fund seven!

We launched a Kickstarter campaign in February 2013 and successfully funded it by 130 percent (raising almost $70,000 between our Kickstarter campaign and on our website). We won the Daily Grommet Challenge in March 2013, beating out 165 other socially conscious products, and we won the Disruptive Innovation Awards in April 2013 from the Tribeca Film Festival! People gravitate to ideas that disrupt the status quo.

We have since acquired a sales rep for the United States and have received distribution inquiries from several countries and regions already (in South America, Canada, the Middle East, Scandinavia, and Australia). Yay!

I am extremely excited to see where this adventure takes us and even more excited to empower women around the world!

The ever-quotable Steve Jobs had a great perspective on the big picture. Reading this quote changed everything for me:

Life can be much broader once you discover one simple fact, and that is, everything around you that you call life was made up by people that were no smarter than you . . . the minute that you understand that you can poke life . . . that you can change it, you can mold it . . . that's maybe the most important thing.

Think about that for a second. Knowing this has given me the power to believe that I can change the rules of my life and be a driving force to make positive change in the way society behaves. You have the power to create things and bring new ideas to the table that can positively affect the way this world operates.

Most people accept their current reality and expect that some governing body or other person with the right title or position will handle their problems, but this rarely happens. We can create new and better rules for society and we have a great opportunity to change the way things are by just choosing to participate and use the power of our voice and our actions.

When it comes to the other important stuff like friendships and romantic partners, it has to be the same way: ever iterating. Otherwise, the relationships grow stale and personal progress isn't made. Both parties have to be willing to evolve and learn. Andrew and I have grown immensely in our quest to constantly improve our romantic relationship. We are open to learn everything we need to please each other. It's never a one-way street, both of us are always willing to listen and grow together without any ego. We let go of all of the things that frustrate us because we know that we are both working hard to become the most actualized versions of ourselves who think about each other.

A great life is an ever-evolving life. Release the nut.

21

TO OUR CHILDREN'S CHILDREN
or, A Message of Encouragement and Empowerment

There are two lasting bequests we can give our children. One is roots.
The other is wings.
—Pulitzer Prize–winning editor Hodding Carter Jr.

Dear future great -grandchildren,
    Thank you for taking the time to read this book!
    When I started to write this final chapter, I grabbed my "box of possibility" from my windowsill and opened it up to go through it. This box holds every single cool memory I've ever had, from tickets to the World Cup in South Africa to invitations to presidential birthday parties to letters from old lovers to plane ticket stubs from all over the world to little trinkets and notes from every adventure and business I'd ever created. And to think that this is just the beginning!
    I recalled that I kept this box for one reason: to remind myself that the *choice* remains in my hands, the choice to continue to do cool shit or not. Do I want this box to be filled with a money, a set of keys to a Rolls-Royce and a boatload of tears because I hate my life, or am I

continuing to fill it with the coolest possible memories I can conjure up on this planet while I am here for a short amount of time? You have the choice of what will go inside *your* box of possibility, so will that change the decisions you make in your life going forward?

I hope that above all else, you learned to put yourself out there in the world and try new things, talk with new people, travel to new places, build a community that inspires you, and create something meaningful, however big or small.

The world of today offers opportunities that did not exist when my parents were growing up, and the world will keep evolving at a faster and faster pace for all generations to come. So just go with it, ride the changing wave with excitement and motivation, and don't resist the change, as it's inevitable. Have fun with it!

A great piece of advice I was told was to always focus on your desired outcome and not the pain you're going through right now to get there, as this desired outcome will keep you inspired and strong, even during your most vulnerable moments.

What has kept me going thus far has been my deep conviction for what I was working on and that it fit the basic requirement of doing cool shit. This means: do what you believe will fulfill your innate being. At the end of the day, if whatever you do does not meet that basic requirement, chances are, it may be "cool" for someone, but not for you.

My dad said to me: "The challenge is to go find what keeps your eyes all sparkling and wide open, and what gets you brushing the dust off your behind every time you fall and come back with greater gusto, and what in your gut feels right without worrying about what the rest of the world in general (or your parents in particular) think about—for rest assured they will come around and they will be your biggest fans and cheerleaders."

So if you have been feeling that itch, that feeling in the pit in your stomach telling you that you are not doing everything you want to be doing, address it now!

We can have all the knowledge, tools, and relationships in the world, but it all comes down to one decision: the decision to *act* and *take your first step* toward doing what you love and living life on your own terms.

And of course doing cool shit is entirely up to your interpretation. The goal here is to find your most authentic voice and give you the motivation to act.

The only way I could have ever gotten here was by acknowledging that I wasn't doing everything that I wanted to and by articulating what I wanted to be doing, so I made a decision to act on making what I wanted to be doing a reality. I realized that at the end of the day, the only person who will be answering to me is *me*.

So go out and do what you believe will fulfill your innate being.

Ask yourself, "What aren't I doing that I want to be?" and realize that there is no time like the present to start doing it.

(ABOUT THE AUTHOR)

Miki Agrawal is a serial social entrepreneur. She is a recipient of the Tribeca Film Festival's Disruptive Innovation Award and was named one of *Forbes* magazine's Top 20 Millienials on a Mission in 2013.

Miki is the founder of the highly acclaimed farm-to-table pizza restaurant *WILD* (www.eatdrinkwild.com), which she opened at age twenty-six in New York City. She partnered has with Zappos.com CEO Tony Hsieh and is opening *WILD Las Vegas*.

She has also partnered with her twin sister, Radha, to launch the Super Sprowtz (www.supersprowtz.com), a multimedia company to get kids excited about eating their vegetables, as a response to the growing obesity pandemic among US children.

Her latest undertaking is THINX (www.shethinx.com), a high-tech underwear solution that is leak- and stain-resistant (and breathable and washable) for girls to wear during their "time of the month." Millions of girls in developing countries drop out of school because of their periods, so for every pair of THINX underwear sold, the company also funds the production of seven washable, reusable cloth pads for girls in developing countries.

Most important, Miki holds the world record for most Wookiee Punches in fifteen seconds, which was broadcast live on *Late Night with Jimmy Fallon* (see the video at recordsetter.com/world-record/punching-wookiee-the-stomach-15-seconds/20056#contentsection).

Miki lives in New York City with Radha.